COTTON AND
SEWING

MAKE YOUR CLOTHES TODAY AND WEAR THEM TOMORROW

CONTENTS

PROJECT GALLERY

No. 30
P.46
Tucked Skirt
Instruction Guide **P.86**

No. 29
P.45
Overalls
Instruction Guide **P.83**

No. 28
P.44
Tucked Pants
Instruction Guide **P.84**

No. 27
P.43
Gaucho Pants
Instruction Guide **P.81**

No. 26
P.42
Gaucho Pants
Instruction Guide **P.81**

OUTER

No. 02
P.06
Double Collarless Coat
Instruction Guide **P.61**

No. 01
P.04
Collarless Coat
Instruction Guide **P.59**

No. 33
P.49
Gathered Button Front Skirt
Instruction Guide **P.87**

No. 32
P.48
Gathered Button Front Skirt
Instruction Guide **P.87**

No. 31
P.47
Tucked Skirt
Instruction Guide **P.86**

No. 07
P.12
Kimono Coat
Instruction Guide **P.14**

No. 06
P.11
Layered Collar Poncho
Instruction Guide **P.65**

No. 05
P.10
Snood Collar Poncho
Instruction Guide **P.64**

No. 04
P.08
Poncho
Instruction Guide **P.62**

No. 03
P.07
Stencil Collar Coat
Instruction Guide **P.59**

No. 40
P.54
Robe Coat
Instruction Guide **P.94**

No. 39
P.53
Ribbed Bolero
Instruction Guide **P.96**

No. 38
P.52
Short Cardigan
Instruction Guide **P.93**

No. 37
P.52
Marguerite
Instruction Guide **P.92**

No. 08
P.13
Kimono Coat
Instruction Guide **P.14-19**

FASHION ITEMS

No. 43
P.55
Snood
Instruction Guide **P.85**

No. 42
P.55
Snood
Instruction Guide **P.85**

No. 41
P.54
Robe Jacket
Instruction Guide **P.94**

Quick to make, beautifully designed haori coats

COLLARLESS COAT

From single-piece coats and ponchos to reversible kimono coats, we will introduce some haori coats that you can make easily before the arrival of winter. Change the fabric, arrange the pieces and create this year's piece.

NO. 01
COLLARLESS COAT

A basic coat with no lining. It gives off a clean, refreshing feeling around the neck and can be worn with a trendy parka. The bold corduroy material gives it a quality appeal that is not too rough.

Instruction Guide **P.61**

Outer fabric: Dyed 6W Corduroy

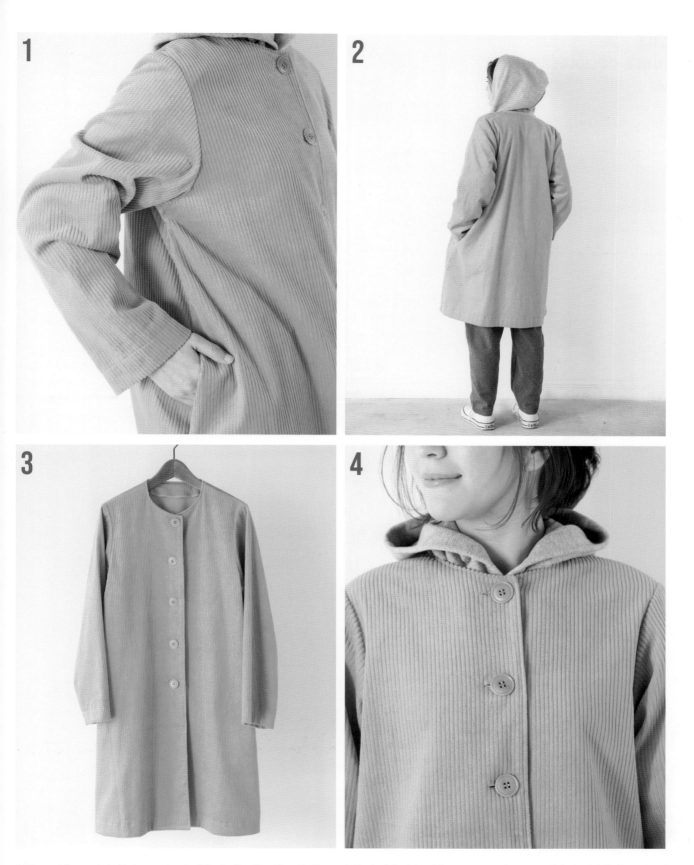

1. The coat has pockets that are cut out of the bodice. Sew the side lines and make the pockets at the same time.

2. The back is plain with no seams at the center of the back. It looks neat and clean.

3. In addition to colored corduroy, wool and linen fabrics can be changed to make it more comfortable, the design can be worn throughout the year.

4. You can choose to have only four buttonholes. You can choose to combine the walnut buttons and the design buttons to make it look good.

NO. 02
DOUBLE COLLARLESS
COAT

The front of No.01 has been deepened to create a double-tailored coat with a feminine line. As there is no collar, it can be worn with a turtleneck top for a crisp look.

Outer fabric: Cable Checkered Tweed

Instruction Guide **P.63**

A single, discreetly attached toggle button provides a single point of presence.

NO. 03
STENCIL COLLAR COAT

We added a collar to No.01 and made it into a wardrobe staple, a stencil collar coat. The basic design is a piece that goes well with any outfit.

Instruction Guide **P.61**

Outer fabric: Synthetic Melton

Made of thick, smooth-touch Melton fabric. Utilizing the right amount of elasticity to create an elegant coat.

NO. 04
PONCHO

A poncho convenient to throw on when it is chilly. As it is collarless, you may wear it with a turtleneck or a shirt.

Instruction Guide **P.64**

Outer fabric: Wool Compressed Jersey

1. The wool compressed jersey has a beautiful finish as the seams are nicely buried in the fabric. It also has a flattering silhouette as it drapes nicely.
3. There are side pockets for added convenience.

2. The V-shaped hem makes the outer garment which has the tendency to look heavy, look neat and light.
4. Backside of the pockets. The left and right pockets are sewn together on the inside of the garment.

NO. 05
SNOOD COLLAR PONCHO

A voluminous faux fur neck piece is added to the poncho in No.04 for a warm outer layer. The sharp image of the windowpane check gives off a soft impression.

Instruction Guide **P.66**

Outer fabric: Yarn-Dyed Wool
Other fabric: Deerskin Boa

The collar that looks like a voluminous snood is perfect for keeping warm. It will be a piece you can't live without this winter.

NO. 06
LAYERED COLLAR PONCHO

This poncho has a classic image with a houndstooth pattern. There is an added layered collar of the same material as No.04 Poncho. The collar, which has a beautiful rise, gives a chic yet not too casual impression.

Instruction Guide **P.67**

Outer fabric: Houndstooth Tweed

The key feature is that the back also has a layered collar.
The style from the side is also elegant and neat.

NO. 07
KIMONO COAT

Reversible kimono coat in a cocoon style. The collar is finished with a dart, and the overall look is a roomy silhouette. The pockets are in the style of a patch pocket. It can be worn in winter with a layered outfit!

Instruction Guide **P.16**

Outer fabric: T/R Long Flocking
Lining fabric: Wool

Reversible tailoring which combines a plain fabric and a modern pattern. The feminine, rounded silhouette is endearing.

NO. 08
KIMONO COAT

This is the same type of kimono coat as No. 07. Since it has an elegant silhouette, it can be paired with denim without giving off an overly rough vibe.

Instruction Guide **P.16 • 21**

Outer fabric: Checkered Plaid Tweed Wool Jacquard,
Lining: Compressed Wool Jersey

A panel line sewn into the waist of No.07 with an in-seam pocket. The overall look is neat and tidy.

★ Before creating the pattern, please refer to Page 59.

How to cut the fabric

※If not specified (figure stated inside the ●), a 1cm seam allowance should be added.

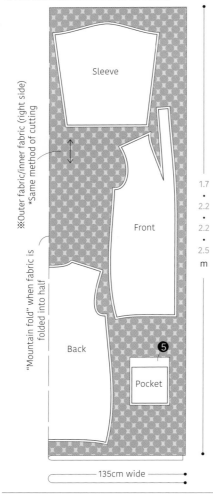

Sleeve

Front

Back

Pocket

❺

※Outer fabric/inner fabric (right side)
*Same method of cutting

"Mountain fold" when fabric is folded into half

1.7
•
2.2
•
2.2
•
2.5
m

135cm wide

No. 07

Page. 14 No. 07 Kimono Coat
Materials

	S	M	L	LL
Outer fabric 135cm wide (Flocking)	1.7m	2.2m	2.2m	2.5m
Inner fabric 135cm wide (Wool Twill)	1.7m	2.2m	2.2m	2.5m
Button 4cm wide	2 pieces			

Sizing

	S	M	L	LL
	100cm	106cm	111cm	116cm
Total length	85cm	88cm	90cm	93cm
Full-scale dress pattern	Side A			

About the pattern

※There is no pattern for the pockets. Please use the following image.
※ Dimensions for ■...S ■...M ■...L ■...LL

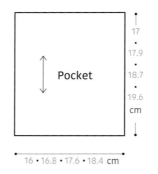

Pocket

17
•
17.9
•
18.7
•
19.6
cm

16 • 16.8 • 17.6 • 18.4 cm

Construction Order

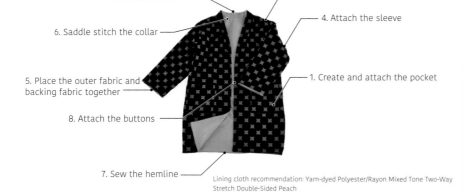

3. Sew the collar

2. Sew the shoulder line

6. Saddle stitch the collar

4. Attach the sleeve

5. Place the outer fabric and backing fabric together

1. Create and attach the pocket

8. Attach the buttons

7. Sew the hemline

Lining cloth recommendation: Yarn-dyed Polyester/Rayon Mixed Tone Two-Way Stretch Double-Sided Peach

---

After cutting

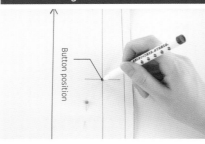

Button position

1. Poke a hole in the pattern for the button and mark the position of the hole with a Chaco pen (also mark the position of the pocket attachment). Remove the pattern and mark the front side of the other sheet in the same manner.

2. Make a 0.5cm notch in the seam allowance for the shoulder line of the collar area, sleeve cap and collar area.
※Be careful not to cut too much.

Back (right side)

3. Remove the pattern paper and put a notch at the back centerline. (Make one on the side of the hem as well.)

1. Create and attach the pocket

Pocket (right side)   Pocket (right side)

1. Sew the seam allowance of the pocket with the overlock (serger) machine (except for the top edge).
※For ease of explanation, the colors of the fabric and yarn have been changed.

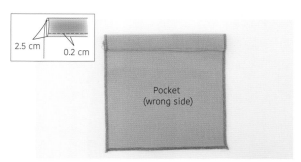

2. Fold the top edge of the seam allowance into three 2.5 cm folds and sew it with the sewing machine.

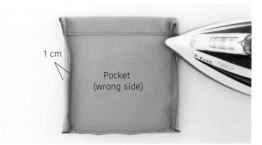

3. Fold the surrounding seam allowance with the iron.

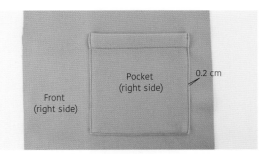

4. Align it to the pocket position and sew around the pocket. Sew the other one in the same manner.

2. Sew the shoulder line

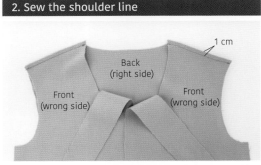

1. Sew the front and back of the coat with the wrong side facing outwards, making sure to align at the shoulder line. Sew using a sewing machine.
※ Wrong side facing outwards: turn the fabric inside out and align it.

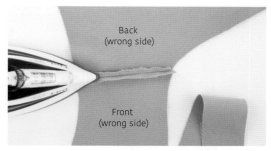

2. Press open the seam allowance with the iron.

3. Sew the collar

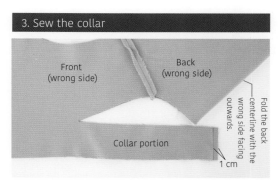

1. Fold the back centerline with the wrong side of the fabric facing outwards, overlap the left and right sides of the front of the coat in the middle of the garment, align the back centerline of the collar, and sew with a sewing machine.

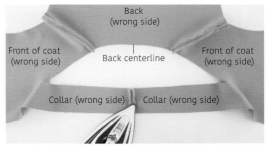

2. Press open the seam allowance with an iron.

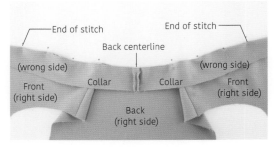

3. Align the back centerline of the body and the back centerline of the collar. Align the collar with the body, and use the sewing pin to hold the end of the stitch of the front of the coat in place.

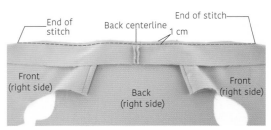

End of stitch — Back centerline — End of stitch
1 cm
Front (right side) — Back (right side) — Front (right side)

4. Use the sewing machine to sew to the end of the stitch.

4. Attach sleeves

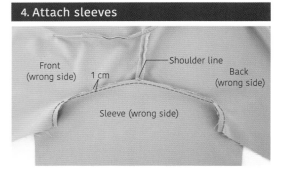

Front (wrong side) — 1 cm — Shoulder line — Back (wrong side)
Sleeve (wrong side)

1. Align the armhole line (of the body) and the line of the sleeve cap (of the sleeve) with the underside of the fabric facing outwards. Sew with the sewing machine.

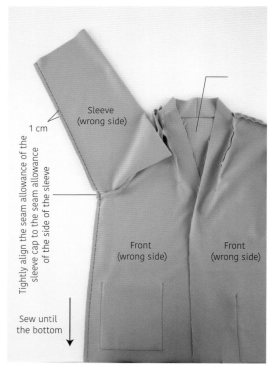

Sleeve (wrong side)
1 cm
Tightly align the seam allowance of the sleeve cap to the seam allowance of the side of the sleeve
Sew until the bottom
Front (wrong side) — Front (wrong side)

2. Align the lower sleeve line, the front and the back side lines with the wrong sides of the fabric facing out. Sew with the sewing machine. Sew the opposite side in the same manner. The inner fabric body is completed.

Outer fabric body (wrong side)

3. In the same manner, create the coat from pieces cut from the outer fabric. (This will be the front of the coat.)

5. Align the outer and inner fabric together.

Match the edges
Outer fabric body (wrong side)
Inner fabric body (wrong side)

1. Place the inner and outer fabric body on top of each other and fasten the edges together with sewing pins.

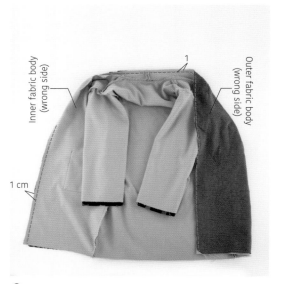

Inner fabric body (wrong side) — 1 — Outer fabric body (wrong side)
1 cm

2. Sew the edges using the sewing machine (leave the hemline).

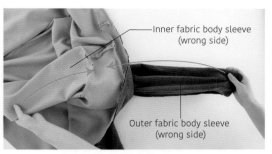

Inner fabric body sleeve (wrong side)

Outer fabric body sleeve (wrong side)

3. Hold the sleeve of the outer body and the sleeve of the inner body. Bring the cuffs together.

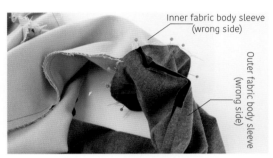

Inner fabric body sleeve (wrong side)

Outer fabric body sleeve (wrong side)

4. Fasten with sewing pins so that the cuff of the outer fabric body and the cuff of the inner fabric body are facing each other. Properly align the seam at the bottom of the sleeve with the mark at the center of the cuff.

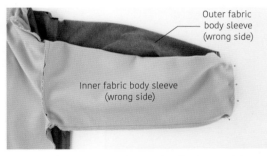

Outer fabric body sleeve (wrong side)

Inner fabric body sleeve (wrong side)

Direct view from the top. Make sure that the sleeves of the inner and outer fabric are not twisted.

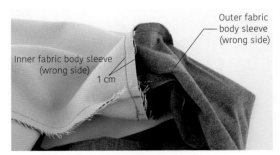

Outer fabric body sleeve (wrong side)

Inner fabric body sleeve (wrong side)

1 cm

5. Sew the cuffs all the way around with the sewing machine.

6. Saddle stitch the collar

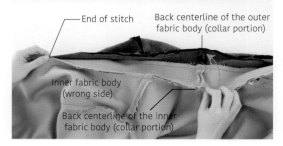

End of stitch

Back centerline of the outer fabric body (collar portion)

Inner fabric body (wrong side)

Back centerline of the inner fabric body (collar portion)

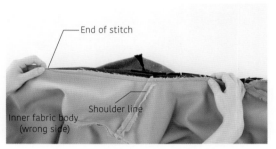

End of stitch

Shoulder line

Inner fabric body (wrong side)

1. With your left hand positioned at the collar end (end of stitch) and your right hand holding the back centerline of the collar, align the seam allowance of the collars of the outer and inner bodies.

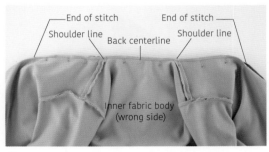

End of stitch   End of stitch

Shoulder line   Back centerline   Shoulder line

Inner fabric body (wrong side)

2. Align until the opposite end and temporarily secure with the sewing pin.

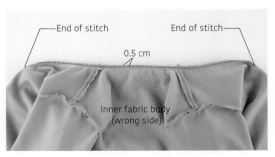

End of stitch   End of stitch

0.5 cm

Inner fabric body (wrong side)

3. Sew the seam allowance outside of the dotted line with the sewing machine (stop slightly before the end of stitch).

7. Sew the hemline

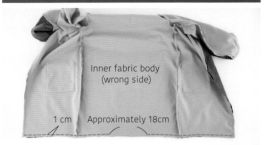

Inner fabric body
(wrong side)

1 cm   Approximately 18cm

1. Align the hemline of the inner and outer fabric of the body (with the wrong side of the fabric facing out), leave an opening for turning and sew the remainder of the hemline.

Inner fabric body
(wrong side)

2. Flip it back to the outer fabric through the opening.

Inner fabric body
(wrong side)

Outer fabric body
(right side)

3. Iron the edges.

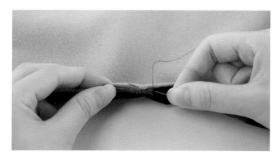

4. Stitch the opening by hand.

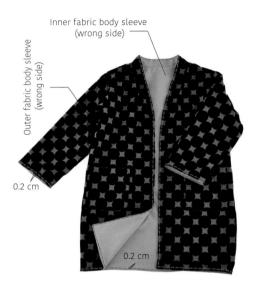

Inner fabric body sleeve
(wrong side)

Outer fabric body sleeve
(wrong side)

0.2 cm

0.2 cm

5. Sew around the edge of the fabric using sewing machine. Sew the cuffs as well.

8. Attach the buttons

Front centerline

Button position

0.3

Length of the buttonhole: width of the button
+
thickness of the button

1. Create a buttonhole and use a ripper to open a hole. Fasten the edges with sewing pins serving as a stopper to prevent from cutting too much. (As it is reversible, make a buttonhole on the front on the right or left per your preference.)

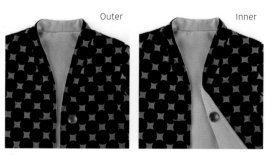

Outer   Inner

2. Attach the button to the button position (both the inner and outer).

※No.08 is based on the pattern from
No.07 arranged as shown in the image below.

※Dimensions for ■…S ■…M ■…L ■…LL

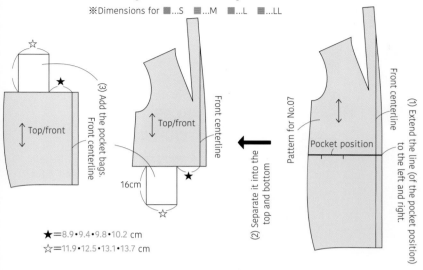

(3) Add the pocket bags.
Front centerline

Top/front

Front centerline

Top/front

Front centerline

16cm

(2) Separate it into the top and bottom

Pattern for No.07

Pocket position

Front centerline

(1) Extend the line (of the pocket position) to the left and right.

★=8.9・9.4・9.8・10.2 cm
☆=11.9・12.5・13.1・13.7 cm

No. 08

Page 13 No.08 Kimono Coat

Materials

	S	M	L	LL
Outer fabric 150cm wide (Wool Tweed)	1.8m	1.9m	2m	2m
Inner fabric 135cm wide (Wool Compressed Jersey)	1.8m	1.9m	2m	2m
Button 4cm wide	2 pieces			

※If using fabric that is soft and stretchy, use 10cm of a 20cm wide interfacing

Sizing

	S	M	L	LL
Bust	100cm	106cm	111cm	116cm
Total length	85cm	88cm	90cm	93cm

Full-scale pattern | Side A

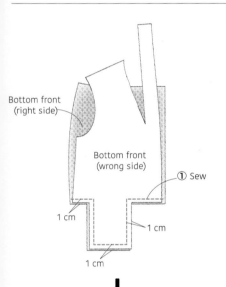

Bottom front (right side)

Bottom front (wrong side)

① Sew

1 cm

1 cm

1 cm

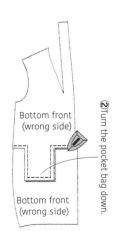

※Sew the other one in the same manner.

Bottom front (wrong side)

② Turn the pocket bag down.

Bottom front (wrong side)

Construction Order

6. Saddle stitch the collar.

3. Sew the collar.

2. Sew the shoulder line

4. Attach the sleeve.

8. Attach the buttons.

1. Sew the panel line.

7. Sew the hemline

5. Place the outer fabric and backing fabric together.

※ For instructions apart from step 1, please refer to pages 16-20.

1. Sew the panel line

--- When using soft and stretchy fabrics ---

① (Please refer to "About sewing knitwear" on Page 60.)

1.5 cm

1.5 cm

3 cm

Bottom front (wrong side)
※2 pieces

▨…Vertical interfacing

How to cut the fabric

※Please add a seam allowance of 1cm.

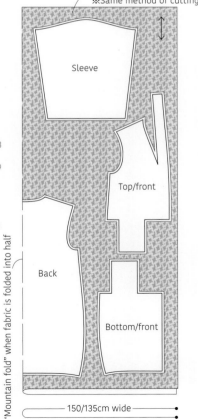

Outer fabric/inner fabric (right side)
※Same method of cutting

Sleeve

Top/front

Back

Bottom/front

1.8
・
1.9
・
2
・
2
m

"Mountain fold" when fabric is folded into half

150/135cm wide

These are the winter clothes that Sakauchi Kyoko, Ito Michiyo, Katayama Yuko and Sewing Pattern Studio would like to introduce to you. There is an array of simple pieces that come with a sense of style that only handmade clothes can bring out.

START MAKING TODAY WHAT YOU WOULD LIKE TO WEAR THIS WINTER

NO.09
TWO-WAY DRESS

A two-way dress with different necklines in the front and back. With the boat neckline in front, you can wear it with a shirt or a cardigan.

Instruction Guide **P.68**

Outer fabric: Wool Compressed Jersey (73648-11, Dark Navy)

The small pockets are a distinct feature.

When worn with the V-neckline in front, the neckline looks neat, and it can be worn with a turtleneck.

NO.10
TWO-WAY VEST

This neckline of the vest is the same as No.09. You can wear it with a turtleneck with the V-neck facing front (photo above) or a shirt with the boat neck facing front (photo below).

Instruction Guide **P.68**

Outer fabric: Boucle Knit Multicolor

NO.11
TWEED DRESS

This tweed-fabric dress has an unstitched pocket opening and a fringe-like feature. The thick texture and elegant glossy weave are eye-catching.

Instruction Guide **P.75**

Outer fabric: Wool Ramel Loop Tweed

NO.12
TWEED PULLOVER

This is the same type of top as No.11 and has loose fringe at the hem and pockets.
The length covers the waist allowing you to wear it with confidence.

Instruction Guide **P.75**

Outer fabric: Tri-Spin Tweed (White)

NO.13
SWEATER PULLOVER

This sweatshirt is made of wide rib material. It also has a wide collar for a feminine neckline and is not too casual.

Instruction Guide **P.70**

Outer fabric: J&B Standard Cotton Combed Yarn Thick Sweatshirt Mixed Oatmeal
Other fabric: Cotton Spun Ribbed Mixed Oatmeal

NO.14
PARKA

No. 14 is No.13's parka with a hood. It is a trendy item for this season, which can be worn with a skirt or a pair of pants. It is thick but very comfortable to the touch as it is made from combed yarn.

Instruction Guide **P.70**

Outer fabric: J&B Standard Cotton
Combed Yarn Thick Sweatshirt Khaki
Other fabric: Cotton Spun Rib

NO.15
HIGH NECK SWEAT PULLOVER

Add a straight neck part to No.13 for a high neck pullover.
Although simple, the ribs on the hem and cuffs are long, so you can wear it in season.

Instruction Guide **P.72**

Outer fabric: Coarsely ground mix fleece border (beige) / mocamocha

NO.16
ROLLED COLLAR PULLOVER

This top is accented with tucked raglan sleeves and a feminine roll collar. White was selected for a clean and elegant look with bold corduroy. It is a piece that will look great with simple coordinates.

Instruction Guide **P.31**

Outer fabric: 8W Corduroy

The rolled collar gives an elegant look to the décolletage at the chest and flattering to the bosom.

The large collar is in the form of a bag-style to express femininity. The cut-out collar from the body accentuates the design.

WHITNEY MUSEUM OF AMERICAN

Richard Diebenkorn, *Ocean Park #125*, 1980   Oil on canvas, 100 x 81 inches

NO.17
RAGLAN SLEEVE PULLOVER

For No.17, the roll collar from No.16 has been removed; it is arranged in a clean, collarless neckline. The plaid print has a strong impact, but the elegance of the grosgrain material complements the design.

Instruction Guide **P.37**

Outer fabric: Slab Grosgrain

NO.18
V-NECK PULLOVER

A pullover with a V-neck that gives a clean, feminine look. It is No. 17 with a collar set in a V shape. The fresh blue color makes the woolly fabric look light and airy.

Instruction Guide **P.37**

Outer fabric: Shaggy Check (h14510)

NO.19
V-NECK DRESS

This is the same type of garment as No.18 with an extended hemline. It can be worn on its own or with denim jeans or tights.

Instruction Guide **P.36**

Outer fabric: Yarn-dyed Polyester, Rayon Two-Way Stretch Double-sided Peach

The back has lovely, crisp lines.

Prepare and cut the pattern

Layer a thin sheet of paper (e.g., Hatron paper) on top of a full-scale pattern and copy the necessary lines from the pattern.

• Marking the necessary lines with an erasable pen such as a friction pen prevents mistakes in copying.

• Place a ruler on a curved line and slide it a little at a time while drawing.

How to attach a seam allowance to the pattern & how to cut the fabric

Seam allowance

Draw the lines for the seam allowance while measuring the seam allowance with a grid ruler.

※If not specified (figure stated inside the ●), a 1cm seam allowance should be added.
※Make a notch where the identifying marks ─ are.
※ denotes the part for attaching the interfacing (please refer to Page 60).

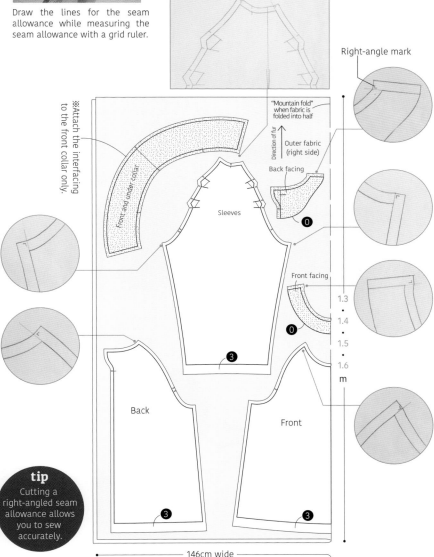

Right-angle mark

"Mountain fold" when fabric is folded into half

Direction of fur

Outer fabric (right side)

Back facing

Sleeves

Front facing

※Attach the interfacing to the front collar only.

Front and under collar

Back

Front

1.3
·
1.4
·
1.5
·
1.6
m

146cm wide

tip
Cutting a right-angled seam allowance allows you to sew accurately.

No. 16

Page 26 No.16 Rolled Collar Pullover

Materials

	S	M	L	LL
Outer fabric 146cm wide (Cotton Corduroy)	1.3m	1.4m	1.5m	1.6m
Interfacing 90cm wide	50cm			
Button 1.8cm wide	1 piece			

Sizing

	S	M	L	LL
Bust	92cm	96cm	101cm	105cm
Total length	57cm	58.5cm	60cm	61.5cm

Full-scale pattern Side C

Construction Order

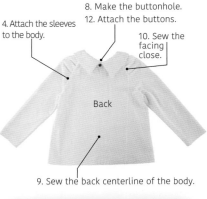

1. Create the facing.
7. Attach the facing to the body.
6. Temporarily attach the collar to the body.
5. Make the collar.
3. Make the sleeves.

Front

11. Sew the hem and cuffs.
2. Sew the side lines of the body.

8. Make the buttonhole.
12. Attach the buttons.
4. Attach the sleeves to the body.
10. Sew the facing close.

Back

9. Sew the back centerline of the body.

tip
• Corduroy should be cut in the direction of smoothness when the fur of the corduroy is stroked upward.
• The collar should be placed between the body and the back facing.

Cut the fabric

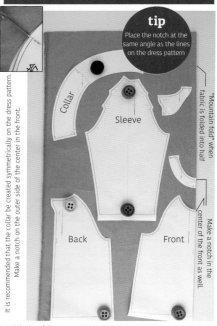

tip
Place the notch at the same angle as the lines on the dress pattern

Fold the fabric and line the dress pattern according to the fabric cutting instructions. After cutting the parts, please make identification marks. Do not forget to cut a notch at the identifying mark in the facing and in the centerline of the front body.

Fabric provided: Polyester Rayon Two-Way Stretch Double-Sided Peach

Sticking the interfacing

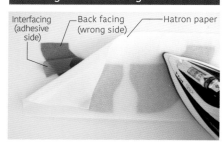

Overlap the interfacing on the wrong side of the facing and iron it. Insert a thin piece of paper (e.g. Hatron paper) to prevent the glue on the interfacing from sticking to the iron.

Sewing machine preparation

tip
By attaching the guide, you can sew straight without marking the fabric.

Measure the width of the seam allowance from the sewing machine needle and attach the guide. A sewing allowance guide or a masking tape would be useful.
sewing allowance guide, Clover Co Ltd

Using the overlock machine

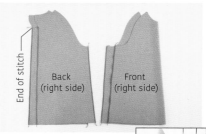

1. Use an overlock machine (or a zigzag sewing machine) to sew on the side lines of the body and the back centerline one piece at a time. Place the right side of the fabric front side up.

2. Use an overlock on the lower sleeveline of the sleeves and the cuffs.

1. Create the facing

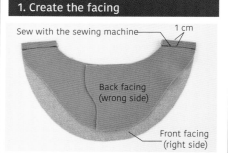

1. Align the front facing and the back facing and sew the shoulder lines.

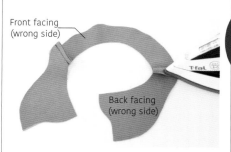

2. Press open the seam allowance.

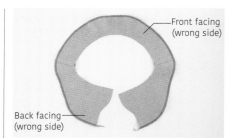

3. Use a an overlock to sew the edges of the facing.

2. Sew the side lines of the body

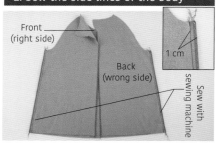

1. Line the front body, the back body and sew the side lines.

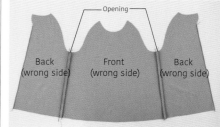

2. Press open the seams.

tip
It is easier to iron a fold into the fabric if you iron while it is flat.

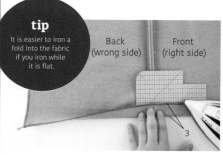

3. Fold the seam allowance of the hem by 3cm. It might help to use an iron ruler.

Iron ruler, Clover Mfg Co Ltd

3. Make the sleeves

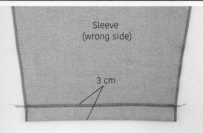

1. Fold the seam allowance of the cuff by 3cm.

2. Check the notches at the positions of the tucks.

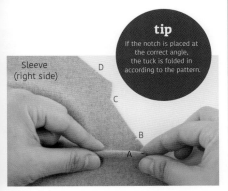

tip
If the notch is placed at the correct angle, the tuck is folded in according to the pattern.

3. Fold the notch at point A into mountain fold. Fold an extension line into the notch.

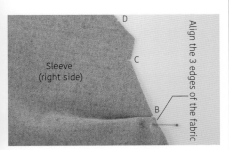

Align the 3 edges of the fabric

4. Align the mountain fold with the notch at point B. Fasten with a sewing pin. If it is folded correctly, the edges of the tucks will be aligned.

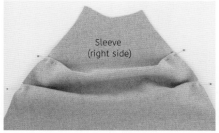

5. As per steps 3 and 4, fold point C and D with the tuck on the back sleeve side and secure with a sewing pin.

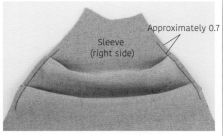

Approximately 0.7

6. Sew the seam allowance with a sewing machine and temporarily secure the tuck.

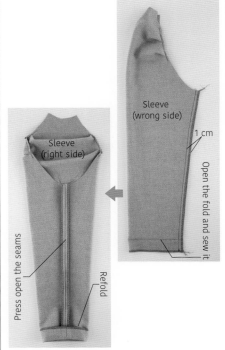

Press open the seams

Refold

Open the fold and sew it

1 cm

7. Sew the bottom line of the sleeves with the machine and press open the seam allowance. Fold the crease of the seam allowance of the cuff and arrange it neatly.

4. Attach the sleeves to the body

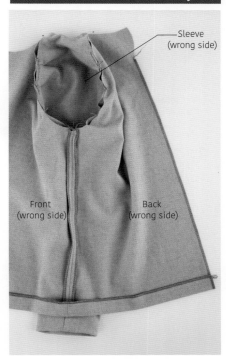

Sleeve (wrong side)

Front (wrong side)   Back (wrong side)

1. Align the sleeve with the body and fasten the armhole with sewing pins.

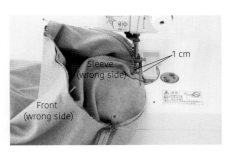

1 cm

Sleeve (wrong side)

Front (wrong side)

2. Sew the armhole with the sewing machine.

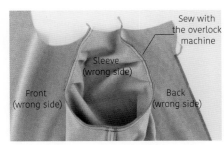

Sew with the overlock machine

Sleeve (wrong side)

Front (wrong side)   Back (wrong side)

3. On the seam allowance of the armhole, use a lockstitch machine to sew both pieces together

5. Make the collar

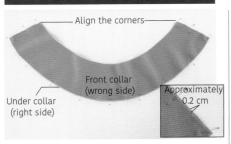

1. Place the two pieces of the collars together and overlap them. Hold the front collar about 0.2cm in and secure it with a sewing pin.

Align the corners
Front collar (wrong side)
Under collar (right side)
Approximately 0.2 cm

5. Perforate the edge.

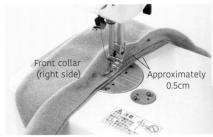

9. With the pins still attached, perforate the corners of the front and under collar. Use the sewing machine to temporarily sew the overlapping seam allowance (Sew as is with the edges out).

Front collar (right side)
Approximately 0.5cm

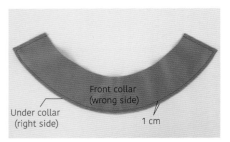

2. Sew the under collar 1cm from the edge of the cloth with the sewing machine.
※ There will be some portion of the front collar left over, but stitch both pieces together while pulling both lightly to absorb the leftover portion from the front collar.

Front collar (wrong side)
Under collar (right side)
1 cm

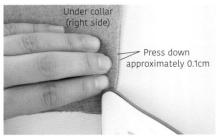

6. Iron the collar from the side of the undercollar and manipulate the fabric so that the under collar is approximately 0.1cm inner than the front collar.

Under collar (right side)
Press down approximately 0.1cm

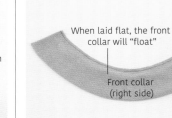

10. The excess amount of fabric on the front collar is the amount needed to make the collar fold over. If this portion is not enough, the collar will curl and the under collar will be visible.

When laid flat, the front collar will "float"
Front collar (right side)

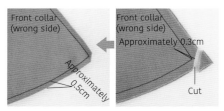

3. Cut the seam allowance at the corner, and cut the seam allowance to approximately 0.5 cm.

Front collar (wrong side)
Front collar (wrong side)
Approximately 0.3cm
Approximately 0.5cm
Cut

6. Temporarily attach the collar to the body

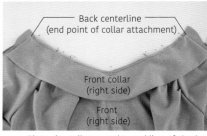

1. Place the collar over the neckline of the body and fasten the edges of the fabric of the under collar and the edge of the body with sewing pins. Fold the seam allowance for the armhole to the side of the sleeve. ※Do not iron the seam allowance; it will fall in different directions depending on the parts, so let it fall naturally.

Back centerline (end point of collar attachment)
Front collar (right side)
Front (right side)

7. When the collar has been adjusted, it will look like this.

Under collar (right side)

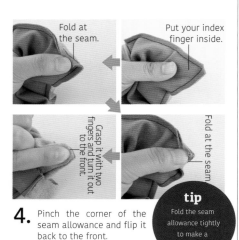

4. Pinch the corner of the seam allowance and flip it back to the front.

Fold at the seam.
Put your index finger inside.
Grasp it with two fingers and turn it out to the front.
Fold at the seam

tip
Fold the seam allowance tightly to make a clean corner.

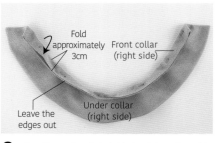

8. Lay the collar flat, fold about 3cm from the collar line, and secure with sewing pins.

Fold approximately 3cm
Front collar (right side)
Leave the edges out
Under collar (right side)

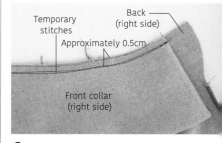

2. Sew temporary stitches into the seam allowance with using the sewing machine.

Temporary stitches
Back (right side)
Approximately 0.5cm
Front collar (right side)

7. Attach the facing to the body

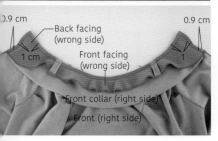

0.9 cm · 0.9 cm
Back facing (wrong side)
1 cm
Front facing (wrong side)
Front collar (right side)
Front (right side)

1. Overlap the facing over the front collar and sew. Sew the back (at the center) where the 0.9cm mark is. For the curved portions, sew 1cm away from the curve.

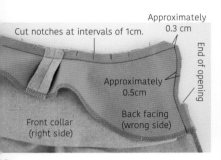

Cut notches at intervals of 1cm.
Approximately 0.3 cm
End of opening
Approximately 0.5cm
Front collar (right side)
Back facing (wrong side)

2. From the end of the opening, cut the seam allowance above to 0.5cm, and cut the seam allowance at the corner as well. Cut notches into the seam allowance of the neckline.

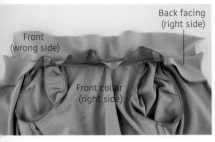

Back facing (right side)
Front (wrong side)
Front collar (right side)

3. Turn the facing over to the right side.

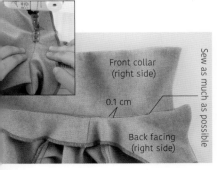

Front collar (right side)
0.1 cm
Back facing (right side)
Sew as much as possible

4. Sew with the seam allowance for the facing and neckline overlapping each other. Avoid the body of the garment, and sew as much as possible.

8. Create the button hole

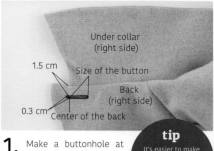

Under collar (right side)
1.5 cm
Size of the button
Back (right side)
0.3 cm
Center of the back

1. Make a buttonhole at the right back with a sewing machine.

tip
It's easier to make the buttonholes when the body is laid flat!

Back (wrong side)

2. Use a pair of cloth scissors to make an incision.

2. Sew 1cm from the edge of the fabric using a zipper foot.

Sew the facing with using sewing machine

3. Sew about 0.1cm to the left of where the facing has been attached using a backstitch. Sew to where the end of the opening is.

9. Sew the back centerline of the body

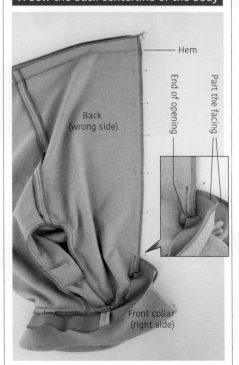

Hem
End of opening
Part the facing
Back (wrong side)
Front collar (right side)

1. Align the outer fabric of the back and fasten the center of the back with sewing pins. Sew in the direction from the hem to the neckline.

10. Sew the facing shut

Back (wrong side)
Press open
Stitch

1. Press open the back center seam allowance with an iron. Stitch the facing onto the seam allowance of the armhole.

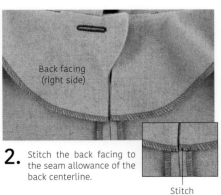

Back facing (right side)
Stitch

2. Stitch the back facing to the seam allowance of the back centerline.

11. Sew the hem and cuffs

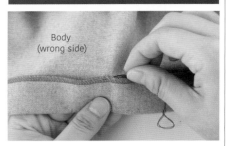

Body
(wrong side)

1. Stitch the hem allowance and the cuffs as well.

12. Attach the button

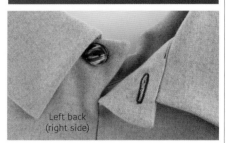

Left back
(right side)

1. Sew the button to the back and on the left.

Finished piece

Front

Back

No. 19

P. 30 No. 19 V-Neck Dress
Materials

	S	M	L	LL
Outer fabric 140cm wide (Polyester Rayon Two-Way Stretch)	1.6m	1.7m	1.8m	2m
Interfacing 90cm wide		30 cm		
Button 1.8cm wide		1 piece		

Sizing

	S	M	L	LL
Bust	92cm	96cm	101cm	105cm
Total length	96cm	98.5cm	101cm	103.5cm

Full-scale pattern | Side C

Construction Order

For the Instruction Guide, please refer to Page 32 to Page 36, excluding instructions for the collar.

1. Create a facing.
8. Sew the facing shut.
5. Attach the facing to the body.
3. Create the sleeves.

Front

9. Sew the hem and cuffs.
6. Create a buttonhole.
4. Attach the sleeves to the body.
10. Attach the button.

7. Sew the back centerline of the body.

Back

2. Sew the side lines of the body.

tip
Although the material is stretchy, it is sewn with regular 60 tex thread.

How to cut the fabric

※If not specified (figure stated inside the ●), a 1cm seam allowance should be added.
※Make a notch where the identifying marks— are.
※ ▨ denotes the part for attaching the interfacing (please refer to Page 60).

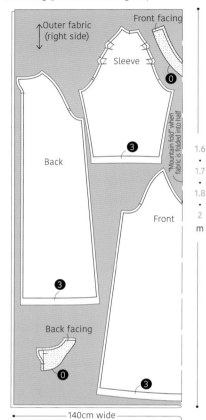

Outer fabric (right side)

Front facing

Sleeve

Back

Front

Back facing

"Mountain fold" when fabric is folded into half

1.6
·
1.7
·
1.8
·
2
m

140cm wide

[How to sew the V-neck]

Apart from the notch in the V-neck, instructions are as per Page 35

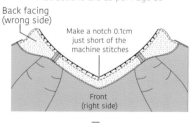

Back facing (wrong side)

Make a notch 0.1cm just short of the machine stitches

Front (right side)

Turn the facing back to the outer fabric. Overlap the seam allowance on the facing and neckline making sure to avoid the body. Sew as much as you can.

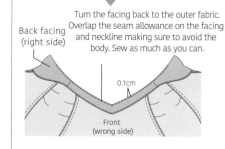

Back facing (right side)

0.1cm

Front (wrong side)

No. 7

P.29 No.17 Raglan Sleeve Pullover

Materials

	S	M	L	LL
Outer fabric 112cm wide (Polyester Slub Grosgrain)	1.6m	1.7m	1.8m	1.9m
Interfacing 90cm wide		30 cm		
Button 1.5cm wide		1 piece		

Sizing

	S	M	L	LL
Bust	92cm	96cm	101cm	105cm
Total length	57cm	58.5cm	60cm	61.5cm

Full-scale pattern   Side C

Construction Order

For the Instruction Guide, please refer to Page 32 to Page 24, excluding instructions for the collar.

1. Create the facing.
8. Sew the facing shut.
5. Attach the facing to the body.
3. Create the sleeves.

Front

9. Sew the hem and cuffs.
6. Create a buttonhole.
10. Attach a button.
4. Attach the sleeves to the body.

Back

2. Sew the side lines of the body.
7. Sew the back centerline of the body.

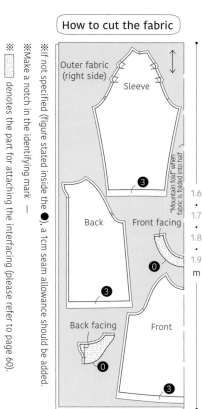

How to cut the fabric

※ denotes the part for attaching the interfacing (please refer to page 60).

※Make a notch in the identifying mark —

※If not specified (figure stated inside the ●), a 1cm seam allowance should be added.

Outer fabric (right side)

Sleeve

"Mountain fold" when fabric is folded into half

Back

Front facing

Back facing

Front

1.6 · 1.7 · 1.8 · 1.9 m

112cm wide

No. 8

P.30 No.18 V-Neck Pullover

Materials

	S	M	L	LL
Outer fabric 138cm wide (Wool Shaggy Check)	1.3m	1.4m	1.5m	1.6m
Interfacing 90cm wide		30 cm		
Button 1.5cm wide		1 piece		

Sizing

	S	M	L	LL
Bust	92cm	96cm	101cm	105cm
Total length	57cm	58.5cm	60cm	61.5cm

Full-scale dress   Side C

tip
Trim the fur in the direction of its smoothness when stroked down.

Construction Order

For the Instruction Guide, please refer to Page 32 to Page 36, excluding instructions for the collar.

1. Create a facing.
8. Sew the facing shut.
5. Attach the facing to the body.
3. Create the sleeves.

Front

9. Sew the hem and cuffs.
6. Create the buttonhole.
10. Attach the button.
4. Attach the sleeve to the collar.

Back

2. Sew the side lines of the body.
7. Sew the back centerline of the body.

How to cut the fabric

※If not specified (figure stated inside the ●), a 1cm seam allowance should be added.
※Make a notch where the identifying marks — are.
※ denotes the part for attaching the interfacing (please refer to Page 60).

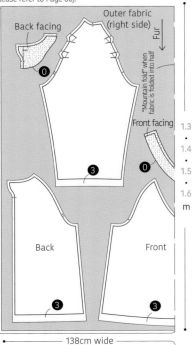

Outer fabric (right side)

Back facing

Fur

"Mountain fold" when fabric is folded into half

Front facing

Back

Front

1.3 · 1.4 · 1.5 · 1.6 m

138cm wide

What you would like for winter?

How about making simple everyday wear in warm winter fabrics?
Wool, knitwear, corduroy, etc..
Find your favorite material and start making clothes.

DAILY WEAR MADE FROM WARM MATERIALS

NO.20
FRENCH SLEEVE TUNIC

The shaggy material and mixed colored check make this dress warm. The French sleeves give you plenty of room for easy layering options.

Instruction Guide **P.78**

Outer fabric: Loop Shaggy Check

material for winter

Shaggy

The word "shaggy" means "furry" in English. As the word implies, it is a material with long fur which feels fluffy. It has a rich, lustrous feel, so your handmade clothes will look a whole lot better.

NO.21
FRENCH SLEEVE PULLOVER

This pullover is a shortened version of the dress in No.20. The knit fabric looks like knitted wool yarn, and comes in handy as a layering piece. The neckline finish varies depending on the material used.

Instruction Guide **P.78**

Outer fabric: Cable Stitch Knit

Knitwear

It is a knitted fabric that stretches and shrinks. For No. 21, we have chosen a slightly thick wool-blend knit fabric that has the texture of woolen yarn knitted with a stick needle. It is stretchy and comfortable to wear. When sewing, a stretchy yarn such as 'Resilon' is recommended.

NO.22
CONTINUOUS SLEEVE TUNIC

A dolman-sleeve tunic with border lines included on the body. It has a relaxed silhouette, but the bouclé fabric gives it an elegant look.

Instruction Guide **P.80**

Outer fabric: Wool Bright Boucle Check

material for winter

Bouclé

Bouclé, which means 'looped' in French, is a recommended winter knitting fabric with fuzzy yarn rings on the surface of the fabric. It is noted for its lightness and warmth, and is often used for cardigans and pullovers in addition to snoods and other accessories.

NO.23
CONTINUOUS SLEEVE PULLOVER

A pullover in the same style as No.22 with a striking check. The generous width of this item encourages you to wear it with style.

Instruction Guide **P.80**

Outer fabric: Dobby Check

material for winter

Dobby

It is a dobby woven fabric. Geometric patterns such as stripes, checks, dots, and flowers are folded into the fabric, giving it a different texture from regular prints. Its luxurious feel is alluring.

NO.24
V-NECK JUMPER SKIRT

The jumper skirt, which can set your style in one piece, is a great choice for the upcoming season. It is a staple to have in your wardrobe. The sharp V-neckline is the key to this piece.

Instruction Guide **P.82**

Outer fabric: Dyed 6W Corduroy

Side View

The large side pockets gives it a style that is not too childish.

material for winter

Corduroy

It is a vertically-ridged cotton fabric. It is used for outerwear, bottoms and socks etc., because it is strong and resistant to friction. The colors of brushed and reverse pile look different. When cutting, all parts should be cut with the pile in a reverse direction.

NO.25
V-NECK JUMPER SKIRT

A jumper skirt with a similar style to No.24 but with a different material. The herringbone material gives it a classical look. Pair it with a shirt or turtleneck.

Instruction Guide **P.82**

Outer fabric: Nep Herringbone

Back View

The back also has a V-neck.

material for winter

Herringbone

A twill weave fabric with an embossed herringbone pattern reminiscent of the bones of herring. In Japan, it is called "sugi herringbone weave". It is often used for men's suits. For women's outerwear and bottoms, it gives a masculine image.

BOTTOMS FOR WINTER

If you prefer everyday wear over elaborate designs, I recommend making rather than buying.

You will love it even more because it is made from your favorite fabric.

Comes with a roomy pocket

NO.26
GAUCHO PANTS

Gaucho pants with a slightly wider hemline silhouette. Elastic waist for easy movement and comfort. It will be a staple piece you can rely on.

Instruction Guide **P.83**

Outer fabric: Yarn-dyed Flannel Stretch Glen Check

NO.27
GAUCHO PANTS

These are the same type of pants as No.26 in a plain stretch material. The slightly shorter length, which shows the ankles, gives a sense of freedom. You can also have some fun by styling with your socks and shoes.

Instruction Guide **P.83**

Outer fabric: Yarn-Dyed Polyester/Rayon Two-Way Stretch Double-sided

The elastic waistband makes the pants comfortable!

NO.28
TUCKED PANTS

Add volume to the pants by tucking in at the waist. It gives the visual of a slimmer waist. The perfect item for a wide range of styles from the casual to the glamourous.

Instruction Guide **P.86**

Outer fabric:T/R Tartan Raised Wool

Keep the front sleek!

Give off a distinct impression from the back as well!

NO.29
OVERALLS

This is a lovely salopette with a V-neck. It is the pants from No. 26 and No. 27 accompanied with an upper body. Designed with a waistline panel for a clean silhouette but it is still comfortable to wear.

Instruction Guide **P.85**

Outer fabric: 8W Corduroy

The V-neck on the back is impressionable!

Side pockets on each side!

NO.30
TUCKED SKIRT

This skirt has a tucked waist as a point of design. Although it has an elastic waistband, tucking reduces the volume around the belly for a sleeker look.

Instruction Guide **P.88**

Outer fabric: Corduroy Shirting

The design at the waist is charming. Dress it well by tucking your top in.

The even-wid tucks are eye catching.

NO.31
TUCKED SKIRT

This skirt is made of a different material from No.30. It is compatible with shirts. The colour hue of this skirt is vivid, and it would look great with darker autumn and winter pieces.

Instruction Guide **P.88**

Outer fabric: Compressed Wool

It is a skirt you will want to make in a variety of colors!

NO.32
GATHERED BUTTON FRONT SKIRT

You can style this skirt in a variety of ways; the side with the button can be worn at the back. It stops at a mid-calf length for a fashionable look.

Instruction Guide **P.89**

Outer Fabric: 30/2 Twill Two-Way Fleece Lining

Change the fabric and it works for all seasons

NO.33
GATHERED BUTTON FRONT SKIRT

This is the same type of skirt as No.32. It is made from finely ridged corduroy. You can style it to be simple yet stylish.

Instruction Guide **P.89**

Outer fabric: Corduroy Shirting

The button cinches the back

WARM WINTER WEAR

"Pattern drafting" might sound a little daunting.
You can make a pattern by drawing a line following the numbers in sequential order for your preferred size. Let us try making a pattern using the simple "pattern drafting" design.

Shape of this top

NO.34
ELBOW-LENGTH PULLOVER

To begin with, this pullover is flat but becomes three-dimensional when worn. It is a piece that can be worn for layering or when it is chilly out. It is convenient to have a piece in your favorite knit fabric.

Instruction Guide **P.90**

Outer fabric: Wool

NO.35
ROLLED KNIT DRESS (S, M, L)

This is a loose and comfortable dress with a rolled collar that looks like a boat neck. Coordinate it with a turtleneck knit or a shirt for a perfect outfit.

Instruction Guide **P.92**

Outer fabric: Wool Nylon

Shape of this top

Shape of this top

NO.36
ROLLED COLLAR KNIT PULLOVER

This is the same type of top as No.35. As it is a roomy pullover, it is suitable for layering with shirts, etc., and can be worn with voluminous bottoms.

Instruction Guide **P.92**

Outer fabric: Wool Nylon

Shape of this top

NO.37
MARGUERITE
(FREE SIZE)

This marguerite cardigan is longer than a bolero. The clean, diamond-shaped lines makes it easy to match with any item.

Instruction Guide **P.94**

Outer fabric: Wool Polyester

Shape of this top

NO.38
SHORT CARDIGAN
(FREE SIZE)

This short length cardigan will make you look more stylish just by throwing it on. It goes well with wide pants and skirts and can be used as a light outer layer.

Instruction Guide **P.95**

Outer fabric: Wool

NO.39
RIBBED BOLERO (S, M, L)

This bolero is accented with long ribbing. It is compact enough to keep in your bag when it is chilly or when the season changes.

Instruction Guide **P.98**

Outer fabric: Wool

Shape of this top

NO.40
ROBE COAT (S, M, L)

A long and easy to wear coat. The large pockets and moderate volume gives it an elegant, edgy look.

Instruction Guide **P.96**

Outer fabric: Jaz Net Wool

Shape of this coat

NO.41
ROBE JACKET (S, M, L)

The rough, thickly knitted fabric of this jacket will elevate your mood for autumn and winter. This item can be worn for a wide range of occasions, from daily outings to commutes.

Shape of this top

Instruction Guide **P.94**

Outer fabric: Cotton Wool Nylon

NO.42
SNOOD

A voluminous snood made from boa material that adorns the neck. The natural twist creates a three-dimensional effect.

Instruction Guide **P.87**

Outer fabric: Polyester Acrylic Boa

Shape of this snood

NO.43
SNOOD

This is a knit snood in the same style as No.42. The snood is indispensable on cold days. It gives off a voluminous look when worn and will add an accent to your fall and winter styling.

Instruction Guide **P.87**

Outer fabric: Wool Acrylic

Shape of this snood

Instruction Guide

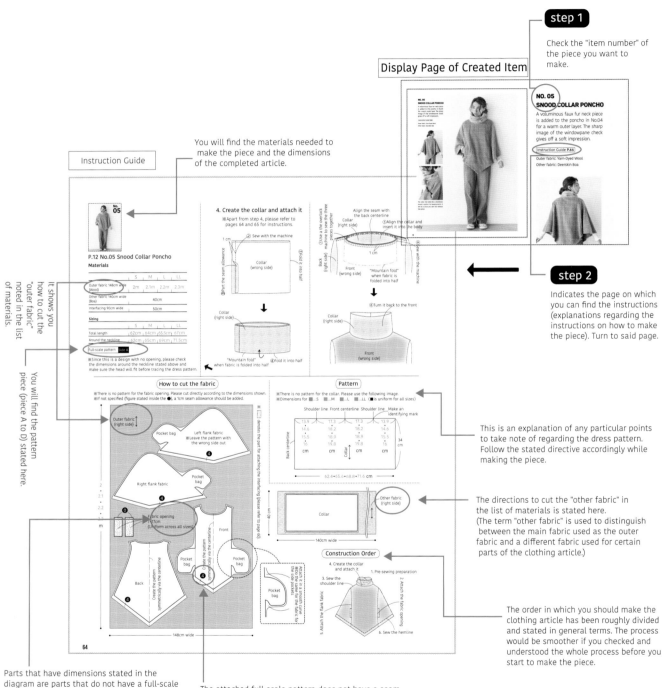

step 1

Check the "item number" of the piece you want to make.

Display Page of Created Item

NO. 05
SNOOD COLLAR PONCHO

A voluminous faux fur neck piece is added to the poncho in No.04 for a warm outer layer. The sharp image of the windowpane check gives off a soft impression.

Instruction Guide P.66

Outer fabric: Yarn-Dyed Wool
Other fabric: Deerskin Boa

Instruction Guide

You will find the materials needed to make the piece and the dimensions of the completed article.

It shows you how to cut the "outer fabric" noted in the list of materials.

You will find the pattern piece (piece A to D) stated here.

P.12 No.05 Snood Collar Poncho
Materials

	S	M	L	LL
Outer fabric 148cm wide (Wool)	2m	2.1m	2.2m	2.3m
Other fabric 140cm wide (Boa)		40cm		
Interfacing 90cm wide		50cm		

Sizing

	S	M	L	LL
Total length	62cm	64cm	65.5cm	67cm
Around the neckline	62cm	65cm	69cm	71.5cm

Full-scale pattern Side A

※Since this is a design with no opening, please check the dimensions around the neckline stated above and make sure the head will fit before tracing the dress pattern.

4. Create the collar and attach it
※Apart from step 4, please refer to pages 64 and 65 for instructions.

② Sew with the machine

Collar (wrong side)

Collar (right side)

"Mountain fold" when fabric is folded into half

④Fold it into half

Align the seam with the back centerline

③Align the collar and insert it into the body

Back (right side)

Front (wrong side)

"Mountain fold" when fabric is folded into half

⑥Turn it back to the front

Collar (right side)

Front (wrong side)

How to cut the fabric

※There is no pattern for the fabric opening. Please cut directly according to the dimensions shown.
※If not specified (figure stated inside the ●), a 1cm seam allowance should be added.

Outer fabric (right side)

Pocket bag

Left flank fabric
※Leave the pattern with the wrong side out

Right flank fabric

Pocket bag

Fabric opening 17cm (Uniform across all sizes)

Front

Create the pattern symmetrically via the centerline

Back

Create the pattern symmetrically via the centerline

Pocket bag

Pocket bag

Pocket bag

148cm wide

64

Pattern

※There is no pattern for the collar. Please use the following image.
※Dimensions for ■..S ■..M ■..L ■..LL (■ is uniform for all sizes)

Shoulder line Front centerline Shoulder line Make an identifying mark

Back centerline

13.9	17.3	17.3	13.9
14.6	18.2	18.2	14.6
15.5	18.9	18.9	15.5
16	19.8	19.8	16
cm	cm	cm	cm

34 cm

62.4・65.6・68.8・71.6 cm

Other fabric (right side)

Collar

140cm wide

Construction Order

4. Create the collar and attach it

3. Sew the shoulder line

1. Pre-sewing preparation

2. Attach the fabric opening

5. Attach the flank fabric

6. Sew the hemline

This is an explanation of any particular points to take note of regarding the dress pattern. Follow the stated directive accordingly while making the piece.

The directions to cut the "other fabric" in the list of materials is stated here.
(The term "other fabric" is used to distinguish between the main fabric used as the outer fabric and a different fabric used for certain parts of the clothing article.)

The order in which you should make the clothing article has been roughly divided and stated in general terms. The process would be smoother if you checked and understood the whole process before you start to make the piece.

step 2

Indicates the page on which you can find the instructions (explanations regarding the instructions on how to make the piece). Turn to said page.

Parts that have dimensions stated in the diagram are parts that do not have a full-scale pattern or drawing instructions. You can cut them by marking them directly on the fabric with an erasable chalk pen or by drawing the pattern on a piece of paper while taking note of the dimensions shown.
Make a pattern with the seam allowance included in the dimensions.

The attached full-scale pattern does not have a seam allowance. When you trace the pattern, use the numbers (stated in a black dot ●) in the "How to cut the fabric" section and add a seam allowance. As for the parts not marked with a black dot, a 1cm seam allowance is usually added. However, this may vary depending on the piece. Therefore, read the notes carefully and follow them.

SIZING

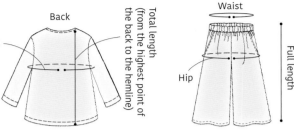

[Reference body measurement for this magazine]

Adult

Reference dimensions	Bust	Waist	Hip	Body measurement	Sleeve length	Rise	Inseam	Height
S	79	61	85.5	37	51.5	25	66	154
M	83	64	90	38	53	26	68	158
L	87	67	94	39	54	26.5	70	162
LL	91	70	98.5	40	55.5	27	71.5	166

How to use the full-scale pattern

step 1 Tear out the full-scale pattern from the magazine.

● From the pattern for the piece of clothing you would like to make, check which side (out of sides) A-D the pattern is on by checking the Instruction Guide.

● Tear the full-scale paper pattern from the magazine by the cut-out lines.

● Check how many colours and how many parts there are on the pattern of the piece you want to make.

● Instructions for arrangements of the necessary items on the pattern are stated on the Instruction Guide, please refer to both for confirmation.

step 2 Tracing the dress pattern

● Place a translucent paper (such as Hatron paper) on top of the dress pattern and copy it with a pencil using a ruler. It is recommended that you use a curve scale for the curves.

● The dress pattern paper does not have a seam allowance. Refer to the diagram on "How to cut the fabric" on the pages of the Instruction Guides and use a grid ruler to add a seam allowance.

● You should also indicate the identifying notches, fabric direction, and the name of the parts.

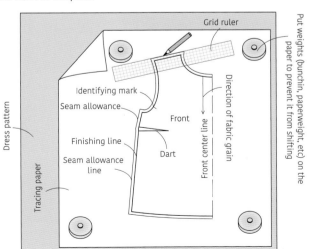

step 3 Cut the pattern

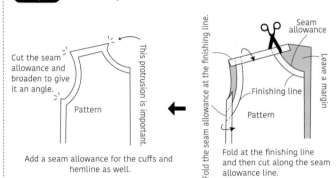

Cut the seam allowance and broaden to give it an angle.

Add a seam allowance for the cuffs and hemline as well.

This protrusion is important.

Fold the seam allowance at the finishing line.

Seam allowance

Leave a margin

Finishing line

Fold at the finishing line and then cut along the seam allowance line.

step 4 Cut

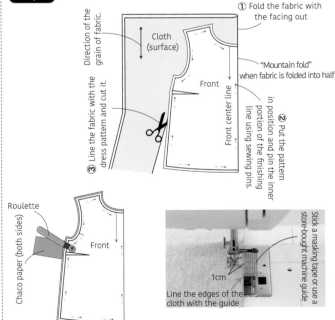

① Fold the fabric with the facing out

"Mountain fold" when fabric is folded into half

② Put the pattern in position and pin the inner portion of the finishing line using sewing pins.

Direction of the grain of fabric.

Cloth (surface)

Front center line

③ Line the fabric with the dress pattern and cut it.

Roulette

Chaco paper (both sides)

Front

1cm

Line the edges of the cloth with the guide

Stick a masking tape or use a store-bought machine guide

⑤For the positioning of the pocket etc., please use Chaco paper and a roulette to make an identifying mark or a dart. ※A notch can be used as an identifying mark.

④ There is essentially no mark for the finishing line. Attach a guide to the sewing machine according to the seam allowance width of the area to be sewn, and sew along it. For example, if you have a 1cm seam allowance, place the guide on the sewing machine 1cm from the needle and sew along it.

How to fuse the interfacing

How to fuse after cutting

Although it is difficult to fuse it onto the fabric perfectly, this method has its advantage in terms of not wasting the interfacing.

(wrong side)

Interfacing

Cut the fabric and the interfacing into the same shape and attach the interfacing to the wrong side of the fabric.

How to cut after attaching the interfacing

It can be affixed more easily as opposed to cutting before fusing.

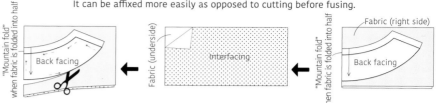

"Mountain fold" when fabric is folded into half

Back facing

Fabric (underside)

Reposition the pattern and cut it.

Interfacing

Cut the interfacing into the same shape as the roughly cut fabric and attach the interfacing to the wrong side of the fabric.

Fabric (right side)

"Mountain fold" when fabric is folded into half

Back facing

Cut a piece of the fabric larger than the part where the interfacing will be fused (rough cut).

About sewing knitwear

Sewing machine needles and sewing thread

Use a sewing machine needle for knit fabrics. The rounded tips of the needles allow you to sew without damaging the knit fabric.

Use "Resilon" sewing thread for knit fabrics. If you use sewing thread for regular fabric, the yarn will not stretch against the stretch of the knit fabric and thread breakage may occur.

About the interfacing

Cut the interfacing for the knit wear and stick it onto the shoulder lines, hems and cuffs etc. Knitwear fabric stretches easily. Therefore, if you do not attach the interfacing, it will stretch and will not look good.
(This method may be used to stop stretching even for regular woven fabrics. In this case, you can use a woven interfacing.)

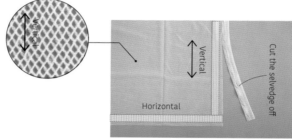

Vertical

Horizontal

Cut the selvedge off

Cut the selvedge off. Add 0.5cm to the seam allowance where the vertical interfacing needs to be pasted. On the seam allowance where the horizontal interfacing is to be attached, cut it into the same width as the seam allowance (if there are instructions in the guide, follow them).
The vertical piece of fabric is used to prevent stretching at the shoulder line, etc., and the horizontal piece of fabric is used where you want it to maintain elasticity yet remain firm.

Direction of stretch

Horizontal

Vertical

Direction of stretch

The horizontal interfacing stretches well lengthwise and the vertical interfacing stretches well breadthwise.

Page 9 No.03 Stencil Coat Collar / About the collar turnover

Add the turnover to the front collar
(use the figure stated on the pattern for the under collar).

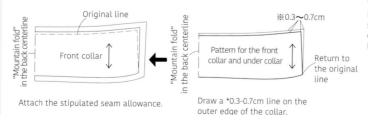

Original line

"Mountain fold" in the back centerline

Front collar

Attach the stipulated seam allowance.

"Mountain fold" in the back centerline

Pattern for the front collar and under collar

※0.3~0.7cm

Return to the original line

Draw a *0.3-0.7cm line on the outer edge of the collar.

※The measurements for the add-on depends on the thickness of the fabric. A rough guide is 0.7cm for thicker materials such as wool, 0.5cm for corduroy and thin wool, and 0.3cm for fabrics such as cotton twill, denim and linen.

What is a collar turnover?

The front collar, which sticks out more when the collar folds back, needs to have a longer right side than the back collar. Therefore, if the front and back collars are the same shape, the material for the front collar will not be sufficient. In doing so, the collar will not fold well and will become taut, making it difficult to keep it in place. For that reason, if you add the turnover to the front collar only, you will get a nice finish.

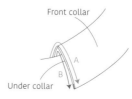

Front collar

A

B

Under collar

Since the length of A (front collar) is longer in relation to B (under collar), the front collar needs to be longer for that portion. Therefore, the thicker the fabric, the larger the difference between A and B.

No. 01 No. 03

.06 No.01 Collarless Coat
.09 No.03 Stencil Collar Coat

Materials

	S	M	L	LL
No.01...Outer fabric 108cm wide (Corduroy) ※Apart from Size S, please use a width of 114cm.	3.1m	3.2m	3.3m	3.3m
No.03...Outer fabric 137cm wide	2.6m	2.7m	3.3m	3.3m
Interfacing 90cm wide		1.1m		
Button 2.5cm wide		5 pieces		

Sizing

	S	M	L	LL
Bust	101cm	106cm	111cm	116cm
Total length	89cm	93.5cm	94cm	96.5cm

Full-scale dress pattern Side A

How to cut the fabric

If not specified (figure stated inside the ●), 1cm seam allowance should be added.

※Add a turnover to the front collar. For more details, please refer to page 60.
※ ▦ denotes the part for attaching the interfacing (please refer to page 60).

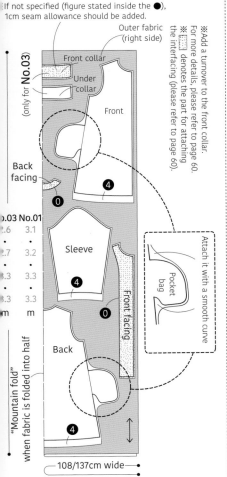

Outer fabric (right side)

Front collar (only for No.03)

Under collar

Front

Back facing

❹ ❺

Attach it with a smooth curve

Pocket bag

Front facing

No.03	No.01
2.6	3.1
2.7	3.2
3.3	3.3
3.3	3.3
m	m

Sleeve

Back

"Mountain fold" when fabric is folded into half

108/137cm wide

Construction Order

3. Create the facing and attach it

1. Pre-sewing preparation

No. 01

2. Sew the shoulder line and side lines

4. Create the sleeves and attach it

5. Attach the button

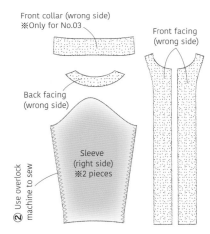

No. 03

※The method of creation is the same for No. 03

1. Pre-sewing preparation

① ▦ denotes the part for attaching the interfacing (please refer to page 60).

Front collar (wrong side) ※Only for No.03

Front facing (wrong side)

Back facing (wrong side)

② Use overlock machine to sew

Sleeve (right side) ※2 pieces

2. Sew the shoulder and side lines

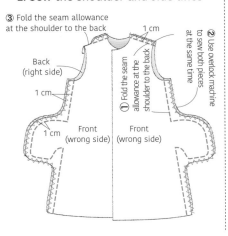

③ Fold the seam allowance at the shoulder to the back

② Use overlock machine to sew both pieces at the same time

① Fold the seam allowance at the shoulder to the back

Back (right side)

1 cm

1 cm

Front (wrong side)

Front (wrong side)

3. Create the facing and attach it

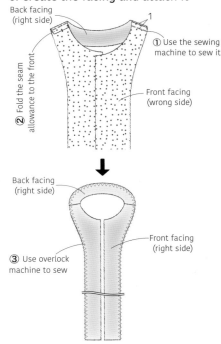

Back facing (right side)

① Use the sewing machine to sew it

② Fold the seam allowance to the front

Front facing (wrong side)

Back facing (right side)

Front facing (right side)

③ Use overlock machine to sew

For No.03, make a collar and temporarily affix it to the body.

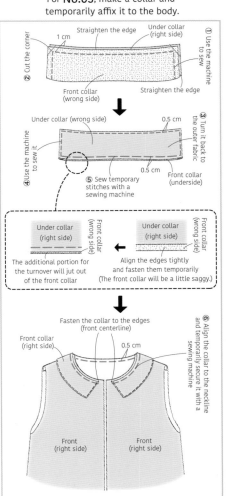

① Use the machine to sew

② Cut the corner

Straighten the edge

1 cm

Under collar (right side)

Front collar (wrong side)

Straighten the edge

③ Turn it back to the outer fabric

④ Use the machine to sew it

Under collar (wrong side)

0.5 cm

0.5 cm

Front collar (underside)

⑤ Sew temporary stitches with a sewing machine

The additional portion for the turnover will jut out of the front collar

Under collar (right side)

Front collar (wrong side)

Under collar (right side)

Front collar (wrong side)

Align the edges tightly and fasten them temporarily (The front collar will be a little saggy.)

⑥ Align the collar to the neckline and temporarily secure it with a sewing machine

Fasten the collar to the edges (front centerline)

Front collar (right side)

0.5 cm

Front (right side)

Front (right side)

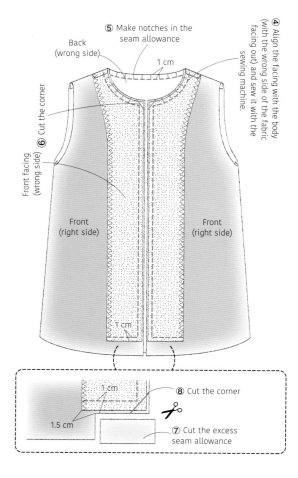

⑤ Make notches in the seam allowance

Back (wrong side)

1 cm

④ Align the facing with the body (with the wrong side of the fabric facing out) and sew it with the sewing machine.

⑥ Cut the corner

Front facing (wrong side)

Front (right side)

Front (right side)

1 cm

⑧ Cut the corner

1 cm

1.5 cm

⑦ Cut the excess seam allowance

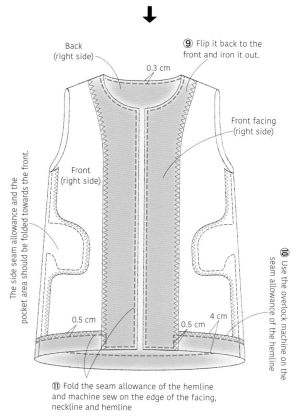

⑨ Flip it back to the front and iron it out.

Back (right side)

0.3 cm

Front facing (right side)

Front (right side)

The side seam allowance and the pocket area should be folded towards the front.

0.5 cm

0.5 cm

4 cm

⑩ Use the overlock machine on the seam allowance of the hemline

⑪ Fold the seam allowance of the hemline and machine sew on the edge of the facing, neckline and hemline

4. Create and attach the sleeve

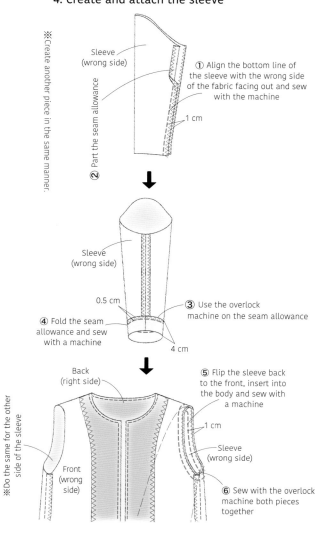

※Create another piece in the same manner.

Sleeve (wrong side)

Part the seam allowance

① Align the bottom line of the sleeve with the wrong side of the fabric facing out and sew with the machine

1 cm

② Part the seam allowance

Sleeve (wrong side)

0.5 cm

④ Fold the seam allowance and sew with a machine

③ Use the overlock machine on the seam allowance

4 cm

Back (right side)

⑤ Flip the sleeve back to the front, insert into the body and sew with a machine

1 cm

Sleeve (wrong side)

Front (wrong side)

⑥ Sew with the overlock machine both pieces together

※Do the same for the other side of the sleeve

5. Attach the button

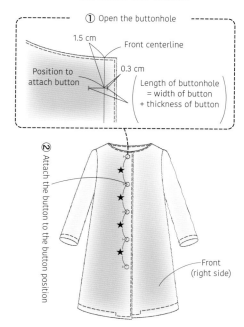

① Open the buttonhole

1.5 cm

Front centerline

Position to attach button

0.3 cm

Length of buttonhole = width of button + thickness of button

② Attach the button to the button position

Front (right side)

★ = Interval between buttons:

11
·
11.3
·
11.5
·
11.8
·
cm

No. 02

P.08 No.02 Double Collarless Coat
Materials

	S	M	L	LL
Outer fabric 160cm wide (Wool Tweed)	2.3m	2.5m	2.5m	2.6m
Interfacing 80cm wide		1.1m		
Toggle button 5.5cm wide		1 piece		
Linen rope 0.5cm wide		50cm		
Snap button 2cm - 2.5cm wide		1 set		

Sizing

	S	M	L	LL
Bust	101cm	106cm	111cm	116cm
Total length	89cm	93.5cm	94cm	96.5cm

Full-scale pattern | Side A

Pattern

※Arrange and use the following image similar to the pattern for No.01

Extend 7cm parallel from the front edge line (uniform across all sizes)

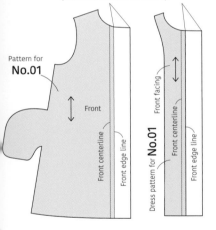

Pattern for **No.01**

Front

Front centerline

Front edge line

Front facing

Front centerline

Front edge line

Dress pattern for **No.01**

Construction Order

3. Create the facing and attach it

1. Pre-sewing preparation

. Create the sleeves and attach it

2. Sew the shoulder and side lines

. Attach the button

How to cut the fabric

How to cut the fabric

※If not specified (figure stated inside the ●), a 1cm seam allowance should be added.

※ ▨ denotes the part for attaching the interfacing (please refer to page 60).

"Mountain fold" when fabric is folded into half

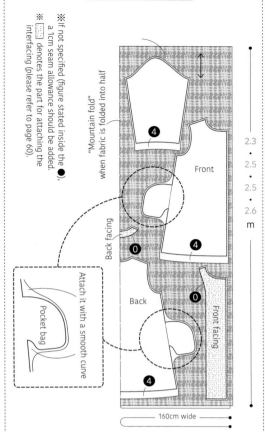

❹

Front

Back facing

❶ ❹

Back

❶

Front facing

Pocket bag

Attach it with a smooth curve

2.3
·
2.5
·
2.5
·
2.6
m

160cm wide

※ Apart from step 5, please refer to pages 61 and 62 for instructions.

5. Attach the button

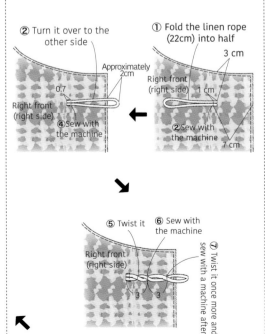

② Turn it over to the other side

Approximately 2cm

0.7

Right front (right side)

④Sew with the machine

① Fold the linen rope (22cm) into half

3 cm

Right front (right side) 1 cm

③ Sew with the machine

7 cm

⑤ Twist it ⑥ Sew with the machine

Right front (right side)

⑦ Twist it once more and sew with a machine after

3 3

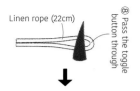

Linen rope (22cm)

⑧ Pass the toggle button through

⑨ Align and overlap with the front centerline
※It should be properly aligned to the bottom so that it does not shift or curl.

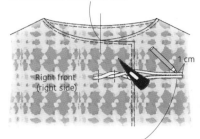

Right front (right side)

1 cm

⑩ Hook the toggle button on the linen rope attached to the right front and mark the right spot (1cm from the inner portion of the rope).

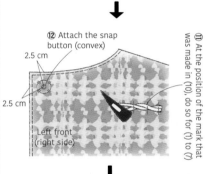

⑫ Attach the snap button (convex)

2.5 cm

2.5 cm

Left front (right side)

⑪ At the position of the mark that was made in (⑩), do so for (1) to (7)

⑬ Use chalk Chaco or colored pencils to color the protrusion in the center of the button (in order to make a mark on the opposite side, a powdery object is easier to make a mark with than an ink-based object)

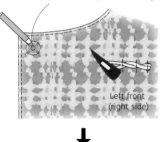

Left front (right side)

⑭ ⑨Align and overlap the front centerline as per (9), use your finger to press the snap button down on the fabric and trace the mark for the location for the concave button.

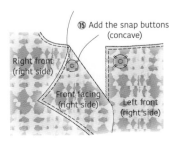

⑮ Add the snap buttons (concave)

Right front (right side)

Front facing (right side)

Left front (right side)

P.10 No.04 Poncho

Materials

	S	M	L	LL
Outer fabric 135cm wide (Wool Compressed Knit)	2m	2.1m	2.2m	2.3m
Interfacing 90cm wide		60cm		

Sizing

	S	M	L	LL
Total	62cm	64cm	65.5cm	67cm
Around the neckline	57.5cm	60.5cm	63.5cm	66cm

Full-scale pattern Side A

※Since this is a design with no opening, please check the dimensions around the neckline stated above and make sure the head will fit before tracing the dress pattern.

Construction Order

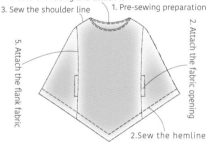

4. Create the facing and attach it
3. Sew the shoulder line
1. Pre-sewing preparation
2. Attach the fabric opening
2. Sew the hemline
5. Attach the flank fabric

1. Pre-sewing preparation

① ┈┈ denotes the part for attaching the interfacing (please refer to page 60).

Fabric opening (wrong side) ※2 pieces
②Use a the overlock machine to sew it

Front facing (wrong side)
Back facing (wrong side)

②Stick the interfacing horizontally on the fabric on the front, back and side fabric (please refer to the portion "About sewing knitwear" on page 60)

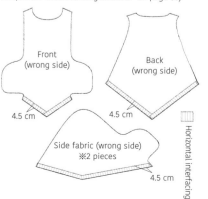

Front (wrong side)   4.5 cm
Back (wrong side)   4.5 cm
Side fabric (wrong side) ※2 pieces   4.5 cm
Horizontal interfacing

How to cut the fabric

Please cut directly according to the dimensions shown.
※If not specified (figure stated inside the ●), a 1cm seam allowance should be added.
※ ▨ denotes the part for attaching the interfacing (please refer to Page 60).

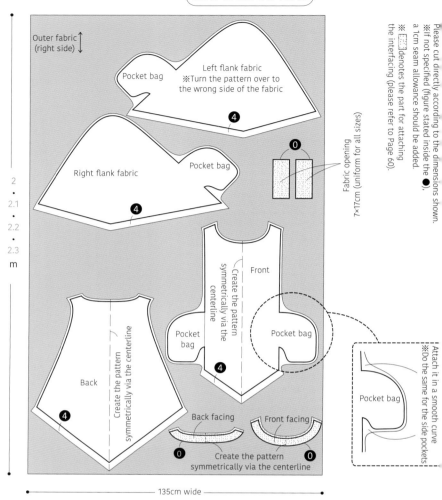

Outer fabric (right side)

Pocket bag
Left flank fabric ※Turn the pattern over to the wrong side of the fabric ❹

❶

Fabric opening
7×17cm (uniform for all sizes)

Right flank fabric   Pocket bag   ❹

Front
Create the pattern symmetrically via the centerline
Pocket bag   Pocket bag   ❹

Back
Create the pattern symmetrically via the centerline ❹

Back facing   Front facing
❶   ❶
Create the pattern symmetrically via the centerline

Pocket bag
Attach it in a smooth curve ※Do the same for the side pockets

2 · 2.1 · 2.2 · 2.3 m

135cm wide

2. Attach a fabric opening

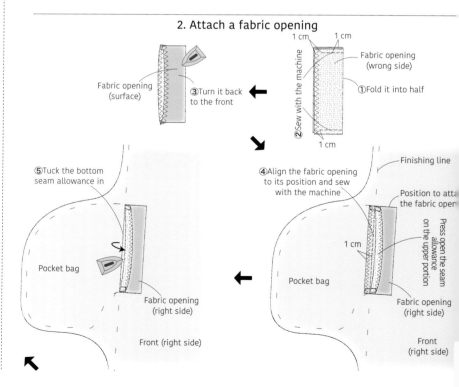

1 cm   1 cm
Fabric opening (wrong side)
②Sew with the machine
①Fold it into half
1 cm

Fabric opening (surface)
③Turn it back to the front

⑤Tuck the bottom seam allowance in
Pocket bag
Fabric opening (right side)
Front (right side)

④Align the fabric opening to its position and sew with the machine
Finishing line
Position to attach the fabric opening
Press open the seam allowance on the upper portion
1 cm
Pocket bag
Fabric opening (right side)
Front (right side)

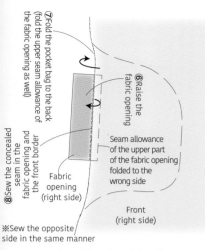

⑦Fold the pocket bag to the back (fold the upper seam allowance of the fabric opening as well)

⑧Sew the concealed seam in the fabric opening and the front border

⑥Raise the fabric opening

Seam allowance of the upper part of the fabric opening folded to the wrong side

Fabric opening (right side)

Front (right side)

※Sew the opposite side in the same manner

3. Sew the shoulder line

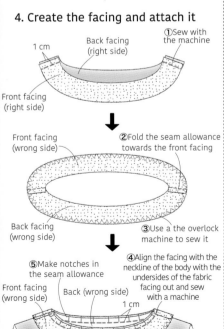

①Sew with the machine

③Fold the seam allowance to the back

1 cm

②Use the overlock sewing machine on both pieces together

Back (right side)

Front (wrong side)

4. Create the facing and attach it

①Sew with the machine

1 cm

Back facing (right side)

Front facing (right side)

②Fold the seam allowance towards the front facing

Front facing (wrong side)

Back facing (wrong side)

③Use a the overlock machine to sew it

⑤Make notches in the seam allowance

④Align the facing with the neckline of the body with the undersides of the fabric facing out and sew with a machine

Front facing (wrong side)

Back (wrong side)

1 cm

Front (right side)

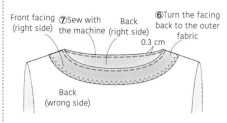

Front facing (right side)

⑦Sew with the machine

Back (right side)

⑥Turn the facing back to the outer fabric

0.3 cm

Back (wrong side)

5. Attach the flank fabrics

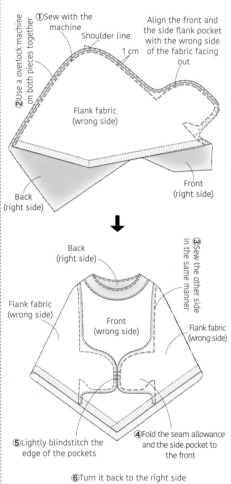

①Sew with the machine

Shoulder line

Align the front and the side flank pocket with the wrong side of the fabric facing out

1 cm

②Use a overlock machine on both pieces together

Flank fabric (wrong side)

Back (right side)

Front (right side)

Back (right side)

③Sew the other side in the same manner

Flank fabric (wrong side)

Front (wrong side)

Flank fabric (wrong side)

⑤Lightly blindstitch the edge of the pockets

④Fold the seam allowance and the side pocket to the front

⑥Turn it back to the right side

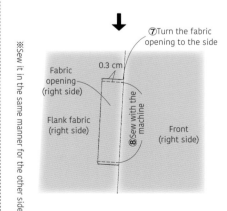

⑦Turn the fabric opening to the side

Fabric opening (right side)

0.3 cm

Flank fabric (right side)

⑧Sew with the machine

Front (right side)

※Sew it in the same manner for the other side

6. Sew the hemline

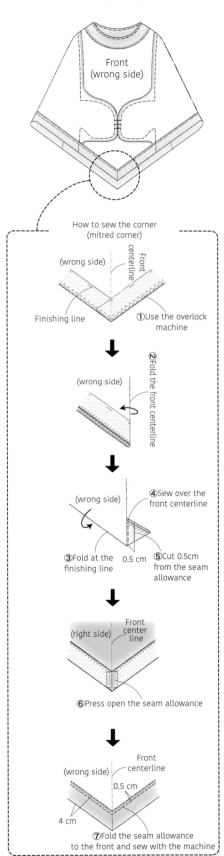

Front (wrong side)

How to sew the corner (mitred corner)

(wrong side)

Front centerline

Finishing line

①Use the overlock machine

(wrong side)

②Fold the front centerline

(wrong side)

④Sew over the front centerline

③Fold at the finishing line

0.5 cm

⑤Cut 0.5cm from the seam allowance

(right side)

Front center line

⑥Press open the seam allowance

(wrong side)

Front centerline

0.5 cm

4 cm

⑦Fold the seam allowance to the front and sew with the machine

P.12 No.05 Snood Collar Poncho

Materials

	S	M	L	LL
Outer fabric 148cm wide (Wool)	2m	2.1m	2.2m	2.3m
Other fabric 140cm wide (Boa)	40cm			
Interfacing 90cm wide	50cm			

Sizing

	S	M	L	LL
Total length	62cm	64cm	65.5cm	67cm
Around the neckline	62cm	65cm	69cm	71.5cm

Full-scale pattern Side A

※Since this is a design with no opening, please check the dimensions around the neckline stated above and make sure the head will fit before tracing the dress pattern.

4. Create the collar and attach it

※Apart from step 4, please refer to pages 64 and 65 for instructions.

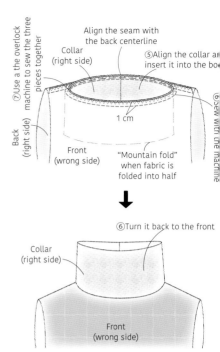

① Fold it into half
② Sew with the machine
③ Part the seam allowance
1 cm
Collar (wrong side)

Collar (right side)

④ Fold it into half
"Mountain fold" when fabric is folded into half

⑦ Use a the overlock machine to sew the three pieces together
Align the seam with the back centerline
Collar (right side)
⑤ Align the collar and insert it into the bod...
Back (right side)
Front (wrong side)
1 cm
"Mountain fold" when fabric is folded into half
⑧ sew with the machine

⑥ Turn it back to the front
Collar (right side)
Front (wrong side)

How to cut the fabric

※There is no pattern for the fabric opening. Please cut directly according to the dimensions shown.
※If not specified (figure stated inside the ●), a 1cm seam allowance should be added.

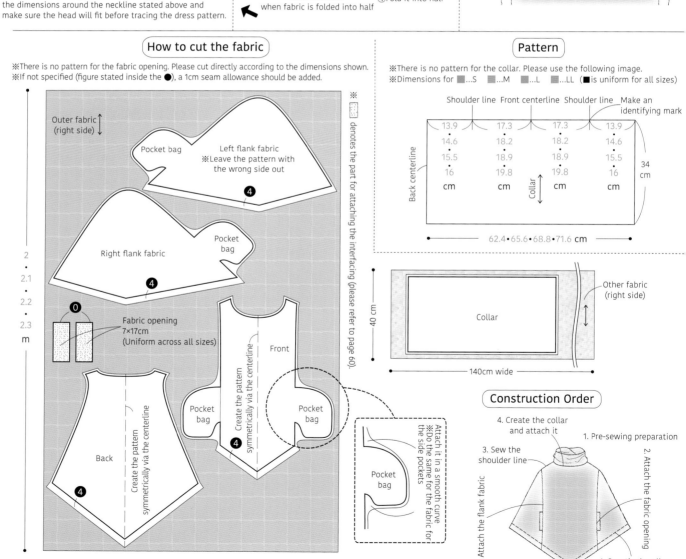

Outer fabric (right side)

※ ⬚ denotes the part for attaching the interfacing (please refer to page 60).

Pocket bag
Left flank fabric ※Leave the pattern with the wrong side out
4

Right flank fabric
Pocket bag
4

2 · 2.1 · 2.2 · 2.3 m

0
Fabric opening 7×17cm (Uniform across all sizes)

Back
Create the pattern symmetrically via the centerline
4

Pocket bag
Front
Create the pattern symmetrically via the centerline
4
Pocket bag

Pocket bag
Attach it in a smooth curve ※Do the same for the fabric for the side pockets

148cm wide

Pattern

※There is no pattern for the collar. Please use the following image.
※Dimensions for ▨...S ▨...M ▨...L ▨...LL (■ is uniform for all sizes)

Shoulder line | Front centerline | Shoulder line | Make an identifying mark

Shoulder line	Front centerline	Shoulder line	
13.9	17.3	17.3	13.9
14.6	18.2	18.2	14.6
15.5	18.9	18.9	15.5
16	19.8	19.8	16
cm	cm	cm	cm

Back centerline
Collar
34 cm

62.4 • 65.6 • 68.8 • 71.6 cm

Other fabric (right side)
Collar
40 cm
140cm wide

Construction Order

4. Create the collar and attach it
1. Pre-sewing preparation
3. Sew the shoulder line
2. Attach the fabric opening
5. Attach the flank fabric
6. Sew the hemline

No. 06

P.13 No.06 Layered Collar Poncho

Materials

	S	M	L	LL
Outer fabric 135cm wide	2m	2.1m	2.2m	2.3m
Interfacing 90cm wide		60cm		

Sizing

	S	M	L	LL
Total length	62cm	64cm	65.5cm	67cm
Around the collar	62cm	65cm	69cm	71.5cm

Full-scale pattern Side A

※Since this is a design with no opening, please check the dimensions around the neckline stated above and make sure the head will fit before tracing the dress pattern.

Construction Order

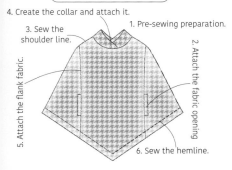

4. Create the collar and attach it.

3. Sew the shoulder line.

1. Pre-sewing preparation.

5. Attach the flank fabric.

2. Attach the fabric opening

6. Sew the hemline.

※ Apart for instructions for step 4, please refer to pages 64 and 65

4. Create the collar and attach it

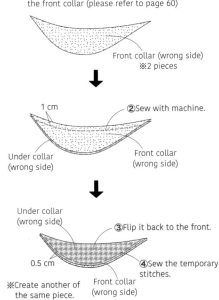

①Stick the interfacing to the wrong side of the front collar (please refer to page 60)

Front collar (wrong side) ※2 pieces

1 cm

②Sew with machine.

Under collar (wrong side)

Front collar (wrong side)

Under collar (wrong side)

③Flip it back to the front.

0.5 cm

④Sew the temporary stitches.

※Create another of the same piece.

Front collar (wrong side)

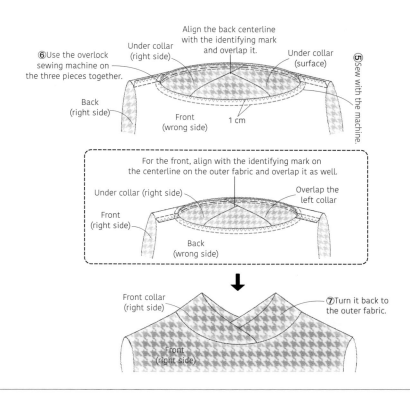

⑥Use the overlock sewing machine on the three pieces together.

Align the back centerline with the identifying mark and overlap it.

Under collar (right side)

Under collar (surface)

⑤Sew with the machine.

Back (right side)

Front (wrong side)

1 cm

For the front, align with the identifying mark on the centerline on the outer fabric and overlap it as well.

Under collar (right side)

Overlap the left collar

Front (right side)

Back (wrong side)

Front collar (right side)

⑦Turn it back to the outer fabric.

Front (right side)

How to cut the fabric

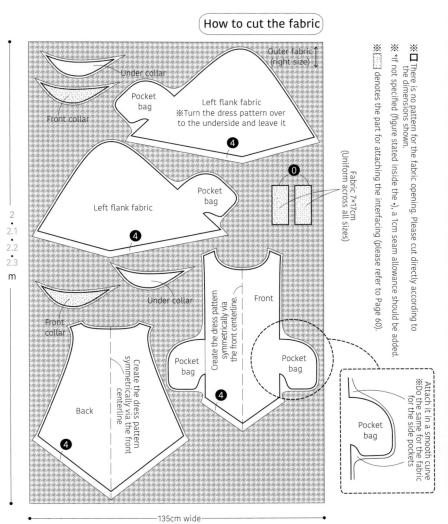

Outer fabric (right size)

Under collar

Pocket bag

Front collar

Left flank fabric ※Turn the dress pattern over to the underside and leave it

4

Left flank fabric

Pocket bag

0

4

Under collar

Front collar

Create the dress pattern symmetrically via the front centerline

Front

Create the dress pattern symmetrically via the front centerline

Pocket bag

Pocket bag

Back

4

4

Fabric 7×17cm (Uniform across all sizes)

Pocket bag

Attach it in a smooth curve ※Do the same for the fabric for the side pockets

2・2.1・2.2・2.3 m

135cm wide

※ ☐ There is no pattern for the fabric opening. Please cut directly according to the dimensions shown.

※ *If not specified (figure stated inside the *), a 1cm seam allowance should be added.

※ ☐ denotes the part for attaching the interfacing (please refer to Page 60).

65

No. 09

No. 10

P.22 No.09 Two-Way Dress

Materials

	S	M	L	LL
Outer fabric 135cm wide (Wool Compressed Jersey)	2.2m	2.3m	2.3m	2.3m
Knit-use interfacing 50cm wide	30cm			

Sizing

	S	M	L	LL
Bust	85.5cm	90cm	94cm	99cm
Total length	100cm	102cm	105cm	108cm

Full-scale pattern **Side B**

P.23 No.10 Two-Way Vest

Materials

	S	M	L	LL
Outer fabric 142cm wide (Boucle Knit)	0.8m	0.8m	0.9m	0.9m
Knit-use interfacing 50cm wide	35cm			

Sizing

	S	M	L	LL
Bust	85.5cm	90cm	94cm	99cm
Total length	54.5cm	56cm	57cm	59cm

Full-scale pattern **Side B**

Construction Order

※Before starting to sew, please read the portion "About sewing knitwear" on page 60.

4. Create the facing and attach it
1. Pre-sewing preparation
3. Sew the shoulder line and armhole.
2.Create the pockets and attach it. (only for No.09)
5. Sew the side lines and hemlines.

No. 09

No. 10

※The same method can be used to make No.10.

How to cut the fabric for No.09

※If not specified (figure stated inside the ●), a 1cm seam allowance should be added.
※ denotes the part for attaching the interfacing (please refer to page 60).

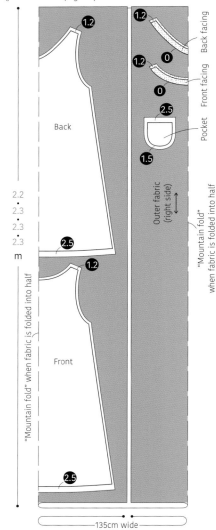

Back facing
Front facing
Pocket
Back
Front
Outer fabric (right side)
"Mountain fold" when fabric is folded into half
"Mountain fold" when fabric is folded into half
2.2 • 2.3 • 2.3 • 2.3 m
135cm wide

How to cut the fabric for No.10

※If not specified (figure stated inside the ●), a 1cm seam allowance should be added.
※ denotes the part for attaching the interfacing (please refer to page 60).

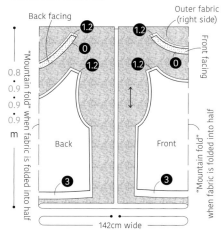

Back facing
Outer fabric (right side)
Front facing
Back
Front
"Mountain fold" when fabric is folded into half
"Mountain fold" when fabric is folded into half
0.8 • 0.9 • 0.9 • 0.9 m
142cm wide

---

1. Pre-sewing preparation

① denotes the part for attaching the interfacing (please refer to page 60).

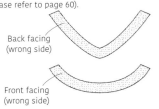

Back facing (wrong side)
Front facing (wrong side)

②Paste a horizontal interfacing onto the armhole and pocket holes. Stick a vertical interfacing on back shoulder line (please refer to page 60).

Horizontal interfacing
Vertical interfacing

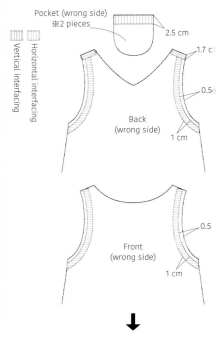

Pocket (wrong side) ※2 pieces
2.5 cm
1.7 c
0.5
Back (wrong side)
1 cm
0.5
Front (wrong side)
1 cm

③Overlock the portion marked ∿∿∿

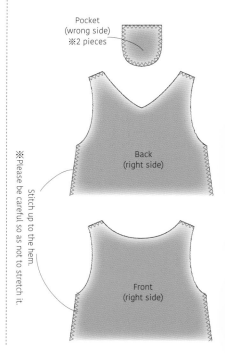

Pocket (wrong side) ※2 pieces
Back (right side)
Front (right side)
Stitch up to the hem.
※Please be careful so as not to stretch it.

66

2. Create the pocket and attach it (only for No.09)

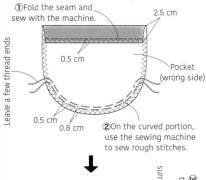

①Fold the seam and sew with the machine.
2.5 cm
0.5 cm
Pocket (wrong side)
Leave a few thread ends
0.5 cm
0.8 cm
②On the curved portion, use the sewing machine to sew rough stitches.

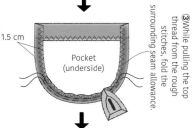

1.5 cm
Pocket (underside)
③While pulling the top thread from the rough stitches, fold the surrounding seam allowance.

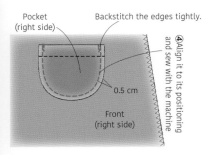

Pocket (right side)
Backstitch the edges tightly.
0.5 cm
Front (right side)
④Align it to its positioning and sew with the machine

※Create the other pocket in the same manner

Sew the shoulder lines and armholes

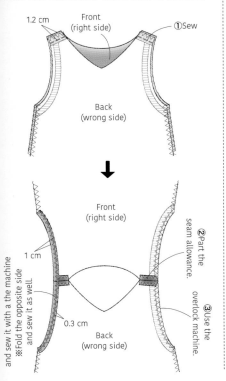

1.2 cm
Front (right side)
①Sew
Back (wrong side)

Front (right side)
1 cm
0.3 cm
Back (wrong side)
②Part the seam allowance.
③Use the overlock machine.
and sew it with a the machine
※Fold the opposite side and sew it as well.

4. Create the facing and attach it

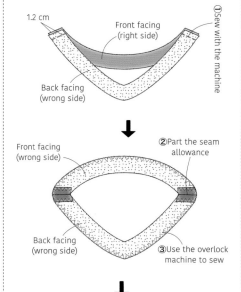

1.2 cm
Front facing (right side)
Back facing (wrong side)
①Sew with the machine

Front facing (wrong side)
②Part the seam allowance
Back facing (wrong side)
③Use the overlock machine to sew

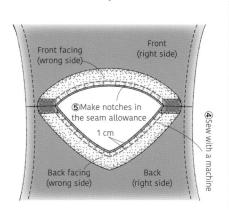

Front facing (wrong side)
Front (right side)
⑤Make notches in the seam allowance
1 cm
Back facing (wrong side)
Back (right side)
④Sew with a machine

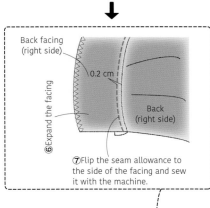

Back facing (right side)
0.2 cm
Back (right side)
⑥Expand the facing
⑦Flip the seam allowance to the side of the facing and sew it with the machine.

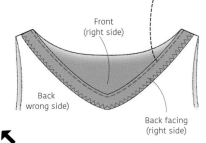

Front (right side)
Back wrong side)
Back facing (right side)

5. Sew the shoulder line and hemline (continued from facing section)

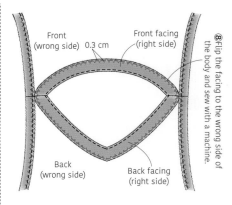

Front (wrong side)
0.3 cm
Front facing (right side)
⑧Flip the facing to the wrong side of the body and sew with a machine.
Back (wrong side)
Back facing (right side)

5. Sew the shoulder line and hemline

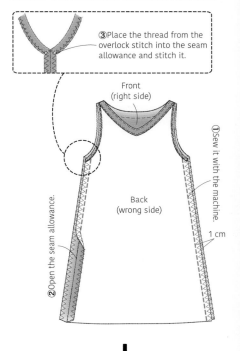

③Place the thread from the overlock stitch into the seam allowance and stitch it.
Front (right side)
Back (wrong side)
①Sew it with the machine.
②Open the seam allowance.
1 cm

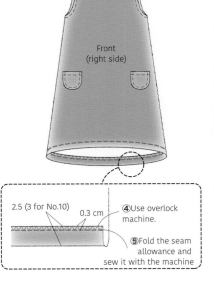

Front (right side)
2.5 (3 for No.10)
0.3 cm
④Use overlock machine.
⑤Fold the seam allowance and sew it with the machine

No. **13**

P.26 No.13 Sweater Pullover

Materials

	S	M	L	LL
Outer fabric 180cm wide (Thick Sweatshirt)	1m	1.1m	1.1m	1.2m
Other fabric 45cm wide (Spun Rib)	0.6m	0.6m	0.6m	0.9m
Knit use interfacing 10cm wide		15cm		

※When the spun rib is folded into a "mountain fold" and laid flat, the width is 45cm. When the "mountain fold" is open as an entire piece, it should measure 90cm.

Sizing

	S	M	L	LL
Bust	94cm	99cm	103cm	108cm
Total length	58cm	59cm	61cm	62cm

Full-scale pattern **Side B**

How to cut the fabric

※Attach a 1cm seam allowance

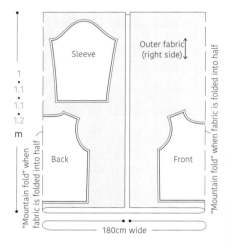

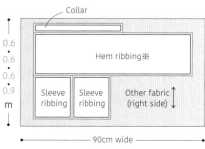

※Open the "mountain fold" so that the fabric is one piece
※For Size LL, there are two pieces for the back hem ribbing and front hem ribbing.

About the pattern

※There is no pattern for the collar, hem ribbing and sleeve ribbing. Please use the image on this page.
※Dimensions for ■...S ■...M ■...L ■...LL (■ is uniform for all sizes)

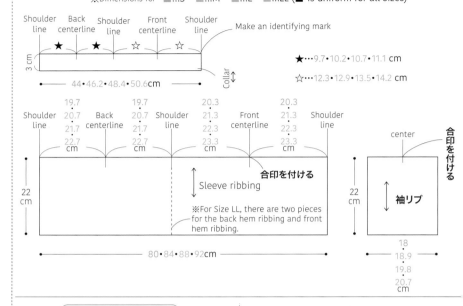

★···9.7・10.2・10.7・11.1 cm
☆···12.3・12.9・13.5・14.2 cm

Construction Order

※Before sewing, please refer to the portion "About sewing knitwear" on page 60.

1. Pre-sewing preparation.
2. Sew the shoulder line.
3. Sew the neckline.
4. Attach the sleeves.
5. Sew the lower sleeve line to the side line.
6. Attach the hem ribbing and sleeve ribbing.

1. Pre-sewing preparation

①Stick a vertical interfacing onto the back of the shoulder line (please refer to page 60)

▓▓▓...Vertical interfacing

2. Sew the shoulder line

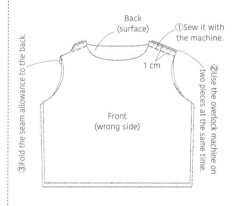

①Sew it with the machine.
②Use the overlock machine on two pieces at the same time.
③Fold the seam allowance to the back.

3. Sew the neckline

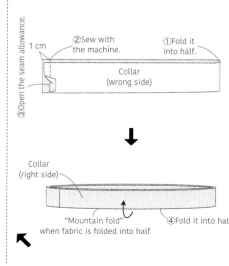

①Fold it into half.
②Sew with the machine.
③Open the seam allowance.
④Fold it into hal
"Mountain fold" when fabric is folded into half

⑤Align the identifying marks on the shoulder line, front and back centerlines to the neckline of the body and pin it.

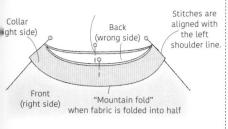

Collar (right side)
Back (wrong side)
Stitches are aligned with the left shoulder line.
Front (right side)
"Mountain fold" when fabric is folded into half

⑥Sew it with the machine
※The collar is shorter than the body. Stretch the collar and sew it to the length of the body.

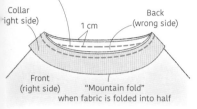

Collar (right side)
1 cm
Back (wrong side)
Front (right side)
"Mountain fold" when fabric is folded into half

⑦Use a the overlock machine on the three pieces together.

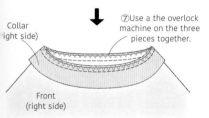

Collar (right side)
Front (right side)

⑧Raise the collar and iron it.

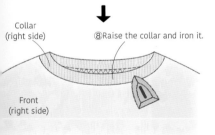

Collar (right side)
Front (right side)

4. Attach the sleeves

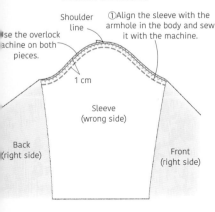

Shoulder line
①Align the sleeve with the armhole in the body and sew it with the machine.
Use the overlock machine on both pieces.
1 cm
Sleeve (wrong side)
Back (right side)
Front (right side)

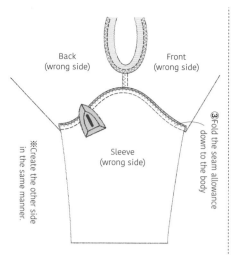

Back (wrong side)
Front (wrong side)
③Fold the seam allowance down to the body
Sleeve (wrong side)
※Create the other side in the same manner.

5. Sew from the lower sleeve line to the side line.

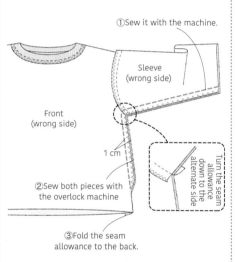

①Sew it with the machine.
Sleeve (wrong side)
Front (wrong side)
1 cm
②Sew both pieces with the overlock machine
Turn the seam allowance down to the alternate side
③Fold the seam allowance to the back.

※Do the same for the opposite side.

6. Attach the hem ribbing and sleeve ribbing

①Create the hem ribbing and the sleeve ribbing in the same manner as the collar.

※For Size LL, sew the rear hem ribbing and front hem ribbing into one piece.

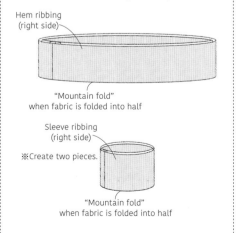

Hem ribbing (right side)
"Mountain fold" when fabric is folded into half
Sleeve ribbing (right side)
※Create two pieces.
"Mountain fold" when fabric is folded into half

②Match the cuffs with the overlapping marks and sew the sleeve ribbing to the length of the sleeves.
③Overlock the three pieces together.

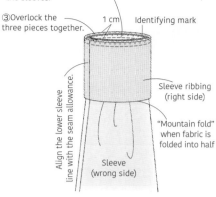

1 cm
Identifying mark
Align the lower sleeve line with the seam allowance.
Sleeve ribbing (right side)
"Mountain fold" when fabric is folded into half
Sleeve (wrong side)

※Sew the other side in the same way

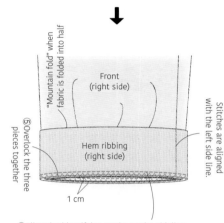

"Mountain fold" when fabric is folded into half
Front (right side)
Stitches are aligned with the left side line.
⑤Overlock the three pieces together
Hem ribbing (right side)
1 cm

④Align the identifying marks on the sideline, front/back centerline that have been overlapped on the hemline, extend the hem ribbing to match the length of the body and sew with the machine.

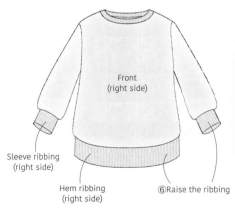

Front (right side)
Sleeve ribbing (right side)
Hem ribbing (right side)
⑥Raise the ribbing

P.27 No.14 Parka

Materials

	S	M	L	LL
Outer fabric 180cm wide (Thick Sweatshirt)	1.2m	1.3m	1.3m	1.4m
Other fabric 45cm wide (Spun Rib)	0.6m	0.6m	0.6m	0.9m
Flat linen string 0.6cm wide		1m		
Knit-use interfacing 10cm wide		20cm		

※For the "mountain-fold of the spun rib, the width should be 45cm when laid flat. When the "mountain-fold" is opened into one piece, the width should be 90cm.

Sizing

	S	M	L	LL
Bust	94cm	99cm	103cm	108cm
Total length	58cm	59cm	61cm	62cm

Full-scale pattern Side B

How to cut the fabric

※If not specified (figure stated inside the ●), a 1cm seam allowance should be added.

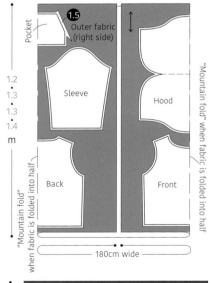

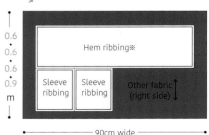

※Open the "mountain-fold" to make it into a single piece.
※For Size LL, there should be a back hem ribbing and a front hem ribbing.

※There is no pattern for the hem ribbing and sleeve ribbing. Please refer to the image on page 70.

About the pattern

[How to attach the seam allowance of the pocket]

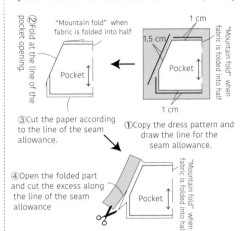

②Fold at the line of the pocket opening.

③Cut the paper according to the line of the seam allowance.

④Open the folded part and cut the excess along the line of the seam allowance

①Copy the dress pattern and draw the line for the seam allowance.

[How to create a hood]

※The pattern of the hood is folded into half in the image below. Make the pattern as shown in the image below.

Fold the copied dress pattern at the upper portion of the position of the "mountain-fold", and cut with a seam allowance around it

Construction Order

※Before sewing, please refer to the "About knit sewing" section on page 60.

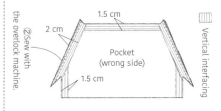

1. Pre-sewing preparation.
2. Create the pocket and attach it.
3. Sew the shoulder line.
4. Create a hood and attach it.
5. Attach the sleeve.
6. Sew the lower sleeve line to the side line.
7. Attach the hem ribbing and the sleeve ribbing.

※ Apart from instructions for step 2 and 4, please refer to pages 70 and 71.

2. Create the pocket and attach it

①Stick the vertical interfacing on the pocket opening, upper edge and the seam allowance of both sides (please refer to page 60)

②Sew with the overlock machine.

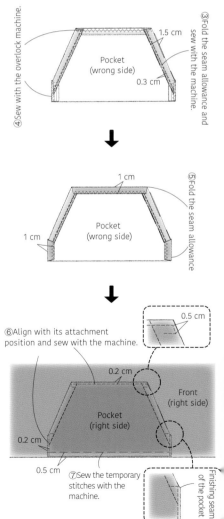

③Fold the seam allowance and sew with the machine.

④Sew with the overlock machine.

⑤Fold the seam allowance

⑥Align with its attachment position and sew with the machine.

⑦Sew the temporary stitches with the machine.

4. Create a hood and attach it

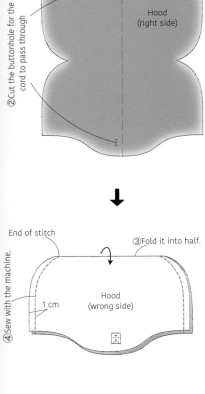

6 cm

1.3 cm

1.5 cm

①Make a marking on the hole where the cord will pass through and stick the interfacing

3 cm

2 cm

Hood (wrong side)

②Cut the buttonhole for the cord to pass through

Hood (right side)

End of stitch

③Fold it into half.

④Sew with the machine.

1 cm

Hood (wrong side)

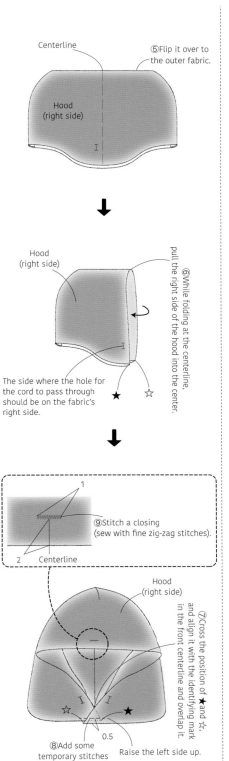

Centerline

⑤Flip it over to the outer fabric.

Hood (right side)

Hood (right side)

⑥While folding at the centerline, pull the right side of the hood into the center.

The side where the hole for the cord to pass through should be on the fabric's right side.

★   ☆

1

⑨Stitch a closing (sew with fine zig-zag stitches).

2   Centerline

Hood (right side)

⑦Cross the position of ★ and ☆, and align it with the identifying mark in the front centerline and overlap it.

⑧Add some temporary stitches

Raise the left side up.

0.5

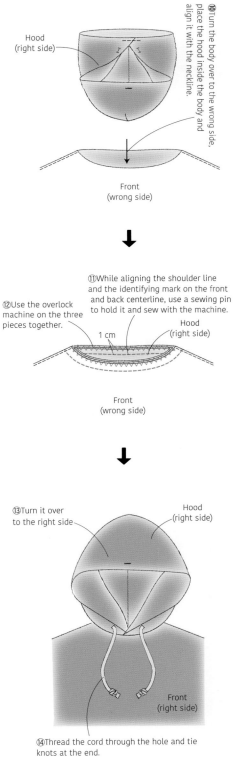

⑩Turn the body over to the wrong side, place the hood inside the body and align it with the neckline.

Hood (right side)

Front (wrong side)

⑪While aligning the shoulder line and the identifying mark on the front and back centerline, use a sewing pin to hold it and sew with the machine.

⑫Use the overlock machine on the three pieces together.

1 cm

Hood (right side)

Front (wrong side)

⑬Turn it over to the right side

Hood (right side)

Front (right side)

⑭Thread the cord through the hole and tie knots at the end.

P.27 No.15 High Neck Sweater Pullover

Materials

	S	M	L	LL
Outer fabric 155cm wide (Raised Wool Border)	1m	1.1m	1.1m	1.2m
Other fabric 45cm wide (Spun Rib)	0.6m	0.6m	0.6m	0.9m
Knit-use interfacing 10cm wide	15 cm			

※The spun rib in its "mountain-fold" position when lying horizontally flat has a width of 45cm. When the "mountain-fold" is open and flat in one piece, it has a width of 90cm.

Sizing

	S	M	L	LL
Bust	94cm	99cm	103cm	108cm
Total length	58cm	59cm	61cm	62cm

Full-scale pattern **Side B**

How to cut the fabric

※Add a seam allowance of 1cm

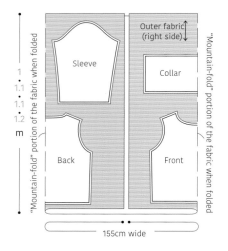

155cm wide

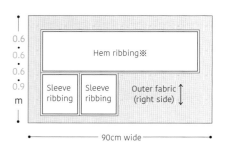

90cm wide

※Open the "mountain fold" so that it is one piece.
※Size LL requires two pieces for the back hem ribbing and the front hem ribbing.

About the pattern

※There are no patterns for the collar, hemline ribbing and the sleeve ribbing.
※Dimensions for ■...S ■...M ■...L ■...LL (■ are uniform)

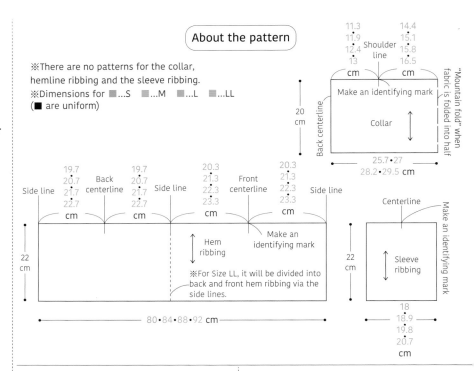

Construction Order

※Before sewing, please refer to the portion "About sewing knitwear" on page 60.

1. Pre-sewing preparation
2. Sew the shoulder line
3. Attach the collar
4. Attach the sleeve
5. Sew the lower sleeve line to the side line
6. Attach the hem ribbing and the sleeve ribbing

※ Apart from step 3, please refer to pages 70 and 71.

3. Attach the collar

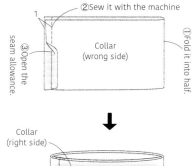

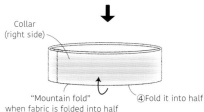

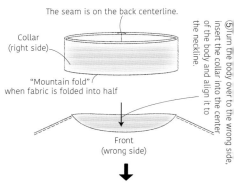

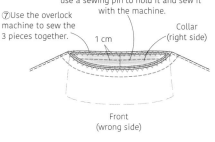

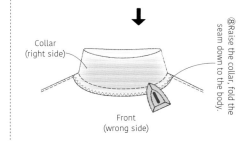

P.22 No.11 Tweed Dress

Materials

	S	M	L	LL
Outer fabric 140cm wide (Loop Tweed)	1.6m	1.6m	2.1m	2.2m
Interfacing 90cm wide		20cm		
Elastic cord 0.3cm wide		5cm		
Button 1cm wide		1 piece		

Sizing

	S	M	L	LL
Bust	94cm	99cm	104cm	108cm
Total length	96cm	99cm	101cm	104cm

Full-scale pattern Side D

P.25 No.12 Tweed Pullover

Materials

	S	M	L	LL
Outer fabric 150cm wide (Tweed)	1.2m	1.3m	1.3m	1.4m
Interfacing 90cm wide		20cm		
Elastic cord 0.3cm wide		5cm		
Button 1cm wide		1 piece		

Sizing

	S	M	L	LL
Bust	94cm	99cm	104cm	108cm
Total length	59cm	60cm	62cm	64cm

Full-scale pattern Side D

How to cut the fabric

※If not specified (figure stated inside the ●), a 1cm seam allowance should be added.
※ ▨ denotes the part for attaching the interfacing (please refer to page 60).

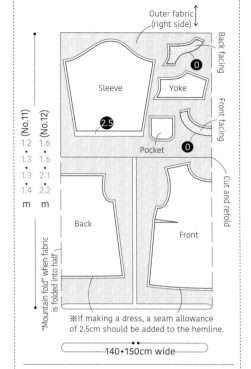

(No.11)	(No.12)
1.2	1.6
1.3	1.6
1.3	2.1
1.4	2.2
m	m

"Mountain fold" when fabric is folded into half

140·150cm wide

※If making a dress, a seam allowance of 2.5cm should be added to the hemline.

1. Pre-sewing preparation

① ▨ denotes the part for attaching the interfacing (please refer to page 60).

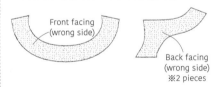

Front facing (wrong side)

Back facing (wrong side)
※2 pieces

---

2. Sew the darts

①Fold the center of the darts with the right side of the fabric facing out, and machine sew where the identifying marks are.

Front (wrong side)

②Turn the seam allowance down.

Front (wrong side)

3. Create the pocket and attach it

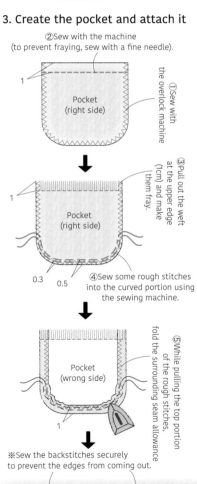

②Sew with the machine (to prevent fraying, sew with a fine needle).

①Sew with the overlock machine

1

Pocket (right side)

③Pull out the weft at the upper edge (1cm) and make them fray.

1

Pocket (right side)

0.3   0.5

④Sew some rough stitches into the curved portion using the sewing machine.

Pocket (wrong side)

⑤While pulling the top portion of the rough stitches, fold the surrounding seam allowance.

1

※Sew the backstitches securely to prevent the edges from coming out.

⑥Align in its positioning and sew it with the machine.

Pocket (right side)

Front (right side)

0.3

※Do the same for the other side.

Construction Order

Back View

6. Sew the panel line in the back

7. Attach the sleeves

9. Finishing

No. 12

5. Create the facing and attach it

1. Pre-sewing preparation

4. Sew the shoulder line

2. Sew the dart

8. Sew from the lower sleeve line to the side line

3. Create the pocket and attach it

No. 11

※The same method can be used to make No.11

4. Sew the shoulder line

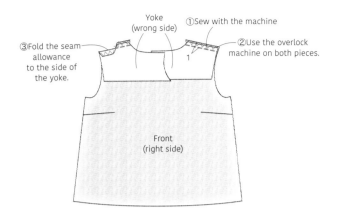

③Fold the seam allowance to the side of the yoke.

Yoke (wrong side)

①Sew with the machine

②Use the overlock machine on both pieces.

1

Front (right side)

5. Create the facing and attach it

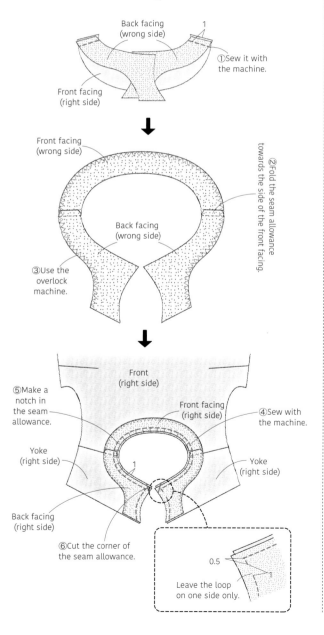

Back facing (wrong side)

1

①Sew it with the machine.

Front facing (right side)

Front facing (wrong side)

Back facing (wrong side)

②Fold the seam allowance towards the side of the front facing.

③Use the overlock machine.

Front (right side)

⑤Make a notch in the seam allowance.

Front facing (right side)

④Sew with the machine.

Yoke (right side)

1

Yoke (right side)

Back facing (right side)

⑥Cut the corner of the seam allowance.

0.5

1

Leave the loop on one side only.

⑦Fold the elastic cord of 4cm into half

2

⑧Insert the leftover sewn portion and use the machine to sew it

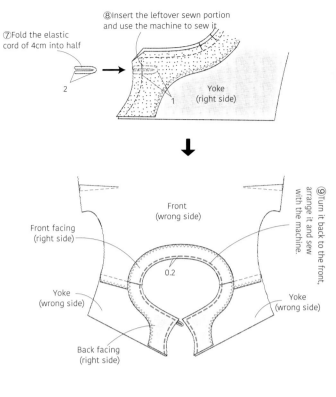

Yoke (right side)

1

⑨Turn it back to the front, arrange it and sew with the machine.

Front (wrong side)

Front facing (right side)

0.2

Yoke (wrong side)

Yoke (wrong side)

Back facing (right side)

6. Sew the panel line in the back

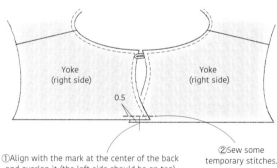

Yoke (right side)

Yoke (right side)

0.5

①Align with the mark at the center of the back and overlap it (the left side should be on top).

②Sew some temporary stitches.

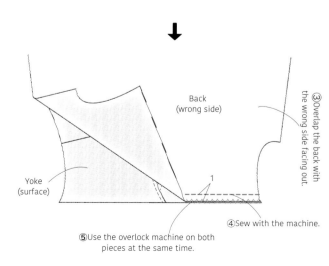

Back (wrong side)

③Overlap the back with the wrong side facing out.

Yoke (surface)

1

④Sew with the machine.

⑤Use the overlock machine on both pieces at the same time.

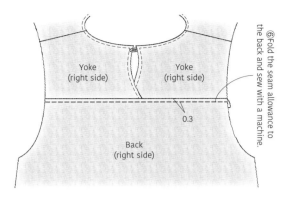

⑥Fold the seam allowance to the back and sew with a machine.

Yoke (right side)   Yoke (right side)

0.3

Back (right side)

7. Attach the sleeves

②Use the overlock machine on the two pieces together.

Shoulder line

①Align the sleeve to the armhole of the body and sew it with the machine.

1

Sleeve (wrong side)

Back (right side)   Front (right side)

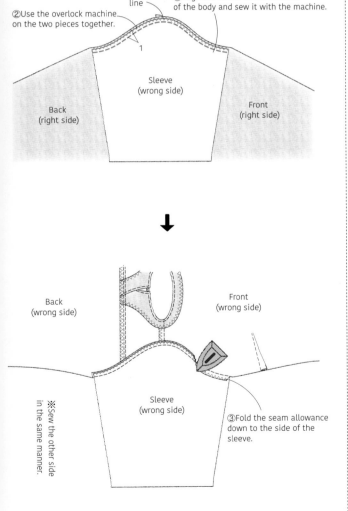

Back (wrong side)   Front (wrong side)

※Sew the other side in the same manner.

Sleeve (wrong side)

③Fold the seam allowance down to the side of the sleeve.

8. Sew the lower sleeve line to the side line

①Sew with the machine.

Sleeve (wrong side)

Front (wrong side)

1

②Use the overlock machine on both pieces together.

③Fold the seam allowance to the back.

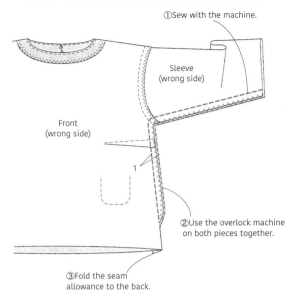

※Sew the other side in the same manner.

9. Finishing

①Attach the button to the back

0.7

0.5

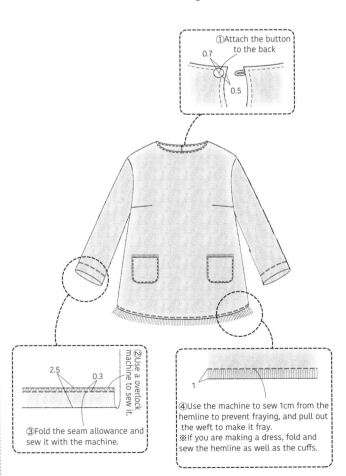

②Use a overlock machine to sew it.

2.5   0.3

③Fold the seam allowance and sew it with the machine.

1

④Use the machine to sew 1cm from the hemline to prevent fraying, and pull out the weft to make it fray.
※If you are making a dress, fold and sew the hemline as well as the cuffs.

P.38 No.20 French Sleeve Tunic

Materials

	S	M	L	LL
Outer fabric 150cm wide (Loop Shaggy)	1.1m	1.1m	1.2m	1.2m
Double-folded bias tape 1.2cm wide	80cm			

※If you use knit fabric, use 10cm of an interfacing of 90cm wide (with no bias tape)

Sizing

	S	M	L	LL
Bust	100cm	105cm	110cm	115cm
Total length	96cm	98cm	101cm	103cm

Full-scale pattern Side C

P.39 No.21 French Sleeve Pullover

Materials

	S	M	L	LL
Outer fabric 140cm wide (Cable Knit Stitch)	0.7m	0.7m	0.8m	0.8m
Interfacing 90cm wide	10cm			

※If you are using a non-stretchy fabric, prepare 80cm of double-sided bias tape that is 1.2cm wide (without any interfacing)

Sizing

	S	M	L	LL
Bust	100cm	105cm	110cm	115cm
Total length	615cm	62.5cm	64.5cm	65.5cm

Full-scale pattern Side D

Construction Order

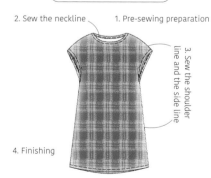

2. Sew the neckline ← 1. Pre-sewing preparation

3. Sew the shoulder line and the side line

4. Finishing

No. 21

※The same method can be used to make No.21.

About the pattern

※For No.21, shorten the pattern used for No.20.

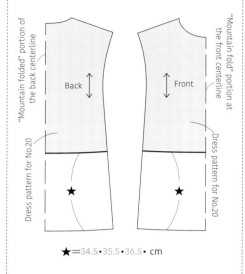

"Mountain folded" portion of the back centerline

"Mountain fold" portion at the front centerline

Back
Front

Dress pattern for No.20

Dress pattern for No.20

★=34.5・35.5・36.5・ cm

How to cut the fabric

※If not specified (figure stated inside the ●), a 1cm seam allowance should be added.

※☆…If using a non-stretchy fabric, use a seam allowance of 0.6cm. If using a knit fabric, use a seam allowance of 1.5cm.

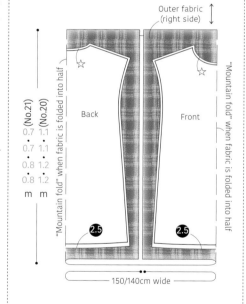

Outer fabric (right side)

	(No.21)	(No.20)
	0.7	1.1
	0.7	1.1
	0.8	1.2
	0.8	1.2
	m	m

Back
Front

"Mountain fold" when fabric is folded into half

2.5
2.5

150/140cm wide

---

1. Pre-sewing preparation

If using knit fabric

①Stick a horizontal interfacing on the neckline, and a vertical interfacing on the front of the shoulder line.

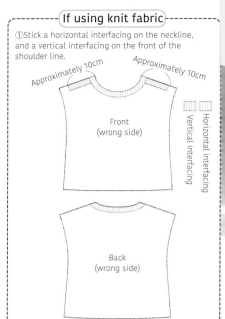

Approximately 10cm Approximately 10cm

Front (wrong side)

Horizontal interfacing
Vertical interfacing

Back (wrong side)

①Overlock the portion marked 〰〰〰

Back (right side)
Front (right side)

2. Sew the neckline

※If using knit material, please proceed to step

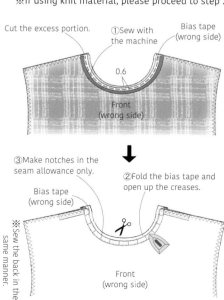

Cut the excess portion.

①Sew with the machine

Bias tape (wrong side)

0.6

Front (wrong side)

③Make notches in the seam allowance only.

Bias tape (wrong side)

②Fold the bias tape and open up the creases.

※Sew the back in the same manner.

Front (wrong side)

3. Sew the shoulder line and side lines

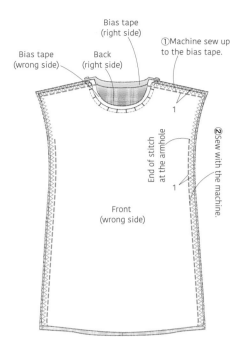

Bias tape (right side)
Bias tape (wrong side)
Back (right side)
①Machine sew up to the bias tape.
1
End of stitch at the armhole
1
②Sew with the machine.
Front (wrong side)

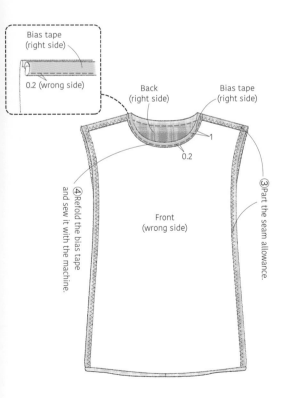

Bias tape (right side)
0.2 (wrong side)
Back (right side)
Bias tape (right side)
1
0.2
④Refold the bias tape and sew it with the machine.
Front (wrong side)
③Part the seam allowance.

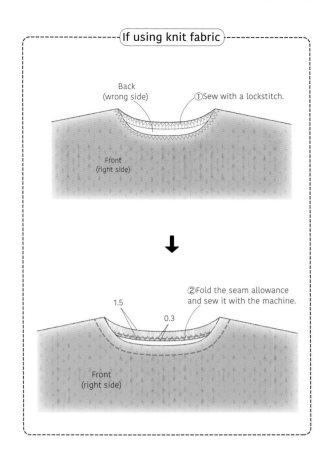

If using knit fabric

Back (wrong side)
①Sew with a lockstitch.
Front (right side)

②Fold the seam allowance and sew it with the machine.
1.5
0.3
Front (right side)

4. Finishing

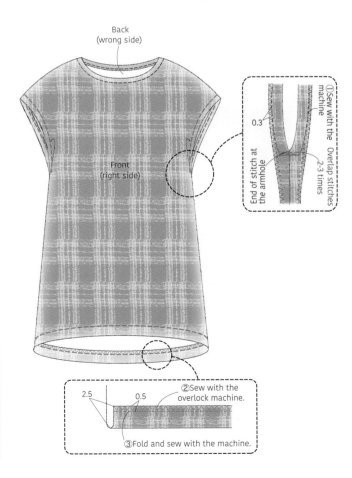

Back (wrong side)
Front (right side)
0.3
End of stitch at the armhole
①Sew with the machine
Overlap stitches 2-3 times
2.5
0.5
②Sew with the overlock machine.
③Fold and sew with the machine.

P.40 No. 22 Continuous Sleeve Tunic

Materials

	S	M	L	LL
Outer fabric 140cm wide (Wool Boucle)	1.9m	2.1m	2.2m	2.2m
Interfacing 90cm wide		30cm		

Sizing

	S	M	L	LL
Bust	133cm	140cm	147cm	153cm
Total length	80cm	82cm	84cm	86cm

Full-scale pattern Side C

P.41 No.23 Continuous Sleeve Pullover

Materials

	S	M	L	LL
Outer fabric 138cm wide (Wool Dobby)	1.5m	1.7m	1.8m	1.8m
Interfacing 90cm wide		30cm		

Sizing

	S	M	L	LL
Bust	133cm	140cm	147cm	153cm
Total length	60.5cm	62cm	63.5cm	65cm

Full-scale pattern Side C

How to cut the fabric

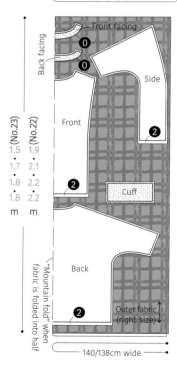

※ If not specified (figure stated inside the ●), a 1cm seam allowance should be added.

※ □□□ denotes the part for attaching the interfacing (please refer to page 60).

(No.23)	(No.22)
1.5	1.9
1.7	2.1
1.8	2.2
1.8	2.2
m	m

140/138cm wide

About the pattern

※For No.23, shorten the dress pattern used for No.22.
※There is no dress pattern for the cuff. Please use the image here.
※ Dimensions for ■...S ■...M ■...L ■...LL (■ is uniform for all sizes)

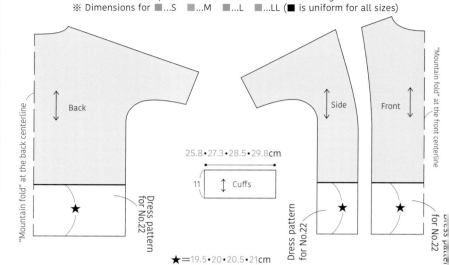

25.8•27.3•28.5•29.8cm

11 ↕ Cuffs

★=19.5•20•20.5•21cm

Construction Order

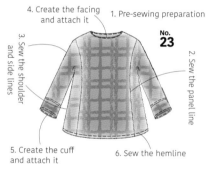

No.
23

4. Create the facing and attach it
1. Pre-sewing preparation
3. Sew the shoulder and side lines
2. Sew the panel line
5. Create the cuff and attach it
6. Sew the hemline

No.
22

※Create No.22 in the same manner.

1. Pre-sewing preparation

① □□□ denotes the part for attaching the interfacing (please refer to page 60).

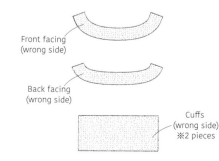

Front facing (wrong side)

Back facing (wrong side)

Cuffs (wrong side) ※2 pieces

2. Sew the panel line

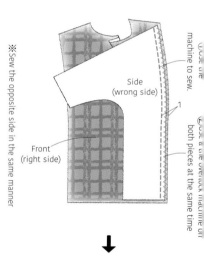

※Sew the opposite side in the same manner.

Side (wrong side)

Front (right side)

↓

③Fold the seam allowance to the front

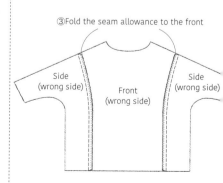

Side (wrong side)

Front (wrong side)

Side (wrong side)

3. Sew the shoulder line and side line

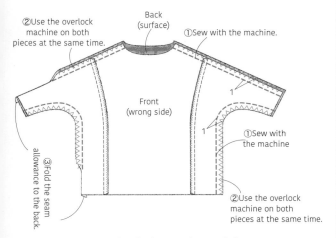

②Use the overlock machine on both pieces at the same time.

Back (surface)

①Sew with the machine.

Front (wrong side)

③Fold the seam allowance to the back.

①Sew with the machine

②Use the overlock machine on both pieces at the same time.

4. Create the facing and attach it

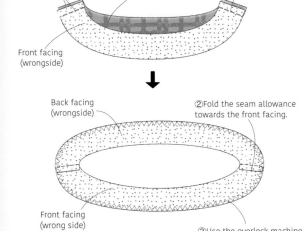

①Sew with the machine

Back facing (right side)

1

Front facing (wrongside)

Back facing (wrongside)

②Fold the seam allowance towards the front facing.

Front facing (wrong side)

③Use the overlock machine

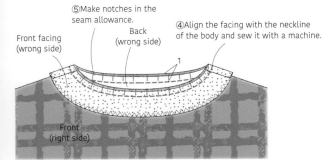

⑤Make notches in the seam allowance.

Back (wrong side)

④Align the facing with the neckline of the body and sew it with a machine.

Front facing (wrong side)

1

Front (right side)

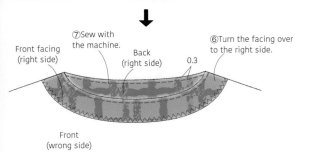

⑦Sew with the machine.

Back (right side)

⑥Turn the facing over to the right side.

Front facing (right side)

0.3

Front (wrong side)

5. Create the cuff and attach it

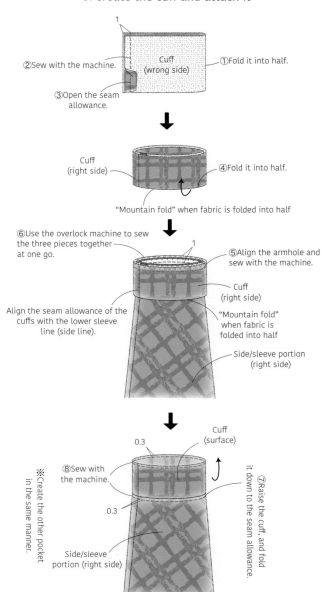

1

②Sew with the machine.

Cuff (wrong side)

①Fold it into half.

③Open the seam allowance.

Cuff (right side)

④Fold it into half.

"Mountain fold" when fabric is folded into half

⑥Use the overlock machine to sew the three pieces together at one go.

1

⑤Align the armhole and sew with the machine.

Cuff (right side)

Align the seam allowance of the cuffs with the lower sleeve line (side line).

"Mountain fold" when fabric is folded into half

Side/sleeve portion (right side)

0.3

Cuff (surface)

⑧Sew with the machine.

0.3

⑦Raise the cuff, and fold it down to the seam allowance.

※Create the other pocket in the same manner.

Side/sleeve portion (right side)

6. Sew the hemline

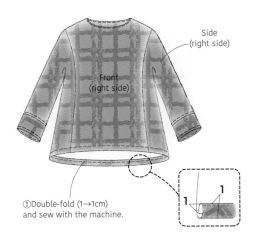

Side (right side)

Front (right side)

①Double-fold (1→1cm) and sew with the machine.

1

1

79

P.42, 43 No.24, No.25 V-Neck Jumper Skirt

Materials

	S	M	L	LL
Outer fabric 108/144cm wide (Corduroy/Wool)	2.4m	2.5m	2.6m	2.6m
Adhesive tape (flat) 1cm wide	1.5m			
Adhesive tape (half-bias) 1cm wide	1.7m			
Double-folded bias tape 1.2cm wide	3.3m			

Sizing

	S	M	L	LL
Bust	90cm	94cm	98cm	103cm
Total length	112cm	115cm	118cm	120.5cm

Full-scale pattern　Side D

[Image]

※There is no dress for the pocket.
Please use the image below.
※Dimensions for ■...S ■...M ■...L ■...LL

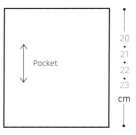

← 17・18・18.9・19.8 cm →

20
21
・
22
23
cm

Construction Order

1. Pre-sewing preparation
4. Sew the centerline/side line
2. Sew the shoulder line
3. Sew the neckline and the armhole
5. Create the pocket
6. Finishing

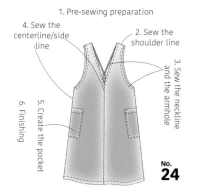

No. 24

No. 25

※Create No.25 in the same manner.

How to cut the fabric

※If not specified (figure stated inside the ●), a 1cm seam allowance should be added.

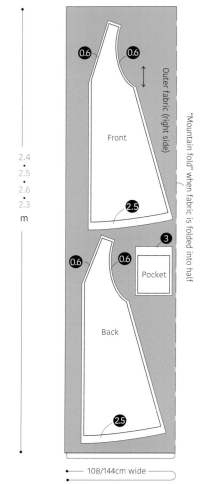

0.6　0.6

Front

Outer fabric (right side)

"Mountain fold" when fabric is folded into half

2.4
・
2.5
・
2.6
・
2.3
m

2.5

3

0.6　0.6

Pocket

Back

2.5

108/144cm wide

1. Pre-sewing preparation

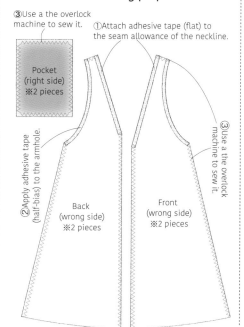

③Use a the overlock machine to sew it.

①Attach adhesive tape (flat) to the seam allowance of the neckline.

Pocket (right side) ※2 pieces

②Apply adhesive tape (half-bias) to the armhole.

③Use a the overlock machine to sew it.

Back (wrong side) ※2 pieces

Front (wrong side) ※2 pieces

2. Sew the shoulder line

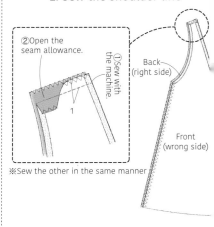

②Open the seam allowance.

①Sew with the machine.

1

Back (right side)

Front (wrong side)

※Sew the other in the same manner.

3. Sew the neckline and the armhole

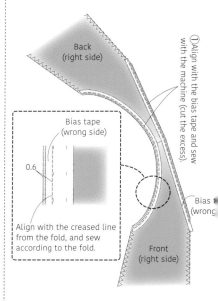

①Align with the bias tape and sew with the machine (cut the excess)

Back (right side)

Bias tape (wrong side)

0.6

Align with the creased line from the fold, and sew according to the fold.

Bias (wrong

Front (right side)

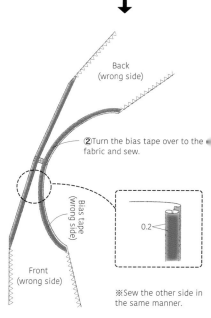

Back (wrong side)

②Turn the bias tape over to the fabric and sew.

Bias tape (wrong side)

0.2

Front (wrong side)

※Sew the other side in the same manner.

4. Sew the centerline/side line

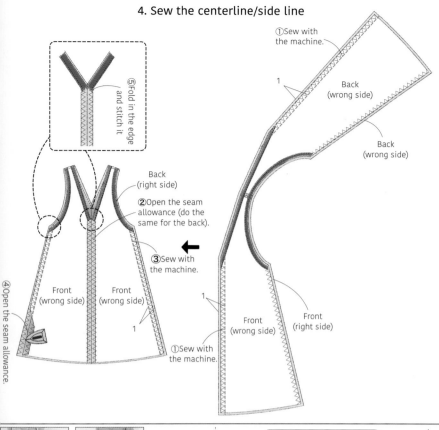

⑤Fold in the edge and stitch it

Back (right side)

②Open the seam allowance (do the same for the back).

③Sew with the machine.

④Open the seam allowance.

Front (wrong side)   Front (wrong side)

1

①Sew with the machine.

①Sew with the machine.

Back (wrong side)

1

Back (wrong side)

1

②Open the seam allowance (do the same for the back).

Front (wrong side)   Front (right side)

1

5. Create the pocket

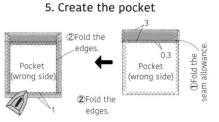

②Fold the edges.

Pocket (wrong side)

3

0.3

②Fold the seam allowance.

Pocket (wrong side)

②Fold the edges.

1

6. Finishing

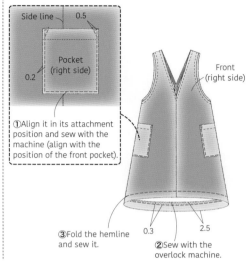

Side line   0.5

Pocket (right side)

0.2

①Align it in its attachment position and sew with the machine (align with the position of the front pocket).

Front (right side)

③Fold the hemline and sew it.

0.3   2.5

②Sew with the overlock machine.

No. 26   No. 27

P.44,45 No.26, No.27 Gaucho Pants

Materials

	S	M	L	LL
Outer fabric 133/140cm wide (Flano/Polyester Rayon)	1.8m	1.8m	1.9m	1.9m
Other fabric 50cm wide (Sheeting)	35cm			
Adhesive tape (flat) 1cm wide	50cm			
Rubber tape 3cm wide	70cm	80cm	80cm	80cm

Sizing

	S	M	L	LL
Waist	67cm	70cm	74cm	77cm
Hip	113cm	119cm	125cm	130cm
Total length	82cm	84cm	86cm	88cm

Full-scale pattern Side D

Construction Order

1. Pre-sewing preparation

2. Create the pocket

3. Sew the side line and the inseam

4. Sew the rise

5. Create the waist belt and attach it

No. 27

6. Finising

No. 26

※Create No.26 in the same manner

How to cut the fabric

※If not specified (figure stated inside the ●), a 1cm seam allowance should be added.

Side fabric

Outer fabric (right side)

Back of pants

❷

Waist belt (1 piece)

Front of pants

❷

"Mountain fold" when fabric is folded into half

"Mountain fold" when fabric is folded into half

1.8
1.8
1.9
1.9
m

133/140cm wide

Other fabric (right side)

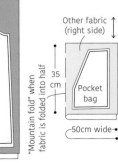

Pocket bag

35 cm

50cm wide

• Refer to the next page for the Instruction Guide.

※There is no pattern for the waist belt. Please use the following image.
※Dimensions for ■...S ■...M ■...L ■...LL (■ is uniform across all sizes)

[Image]

Left side line   Front centerline   Right side line   Back centerline   Left side line

Waist belt   Folded crease line   8cm

98・102・106・110cm

1. Pre-sewing preparation

①Stick the adhesive tape onto the opening of the pocket.

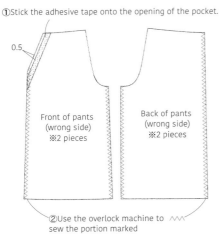

0.5

Front of pants
(wrong side)
※2 pieces

Back of pants
(wrong side)
※2 pieces

②Use the overlock machine to
sew the portion marked ∧∧∧

2. Create the pocket

①Sew with
the machine.

1

Pocket bag
(wrong side)

Front of pants
(right side)

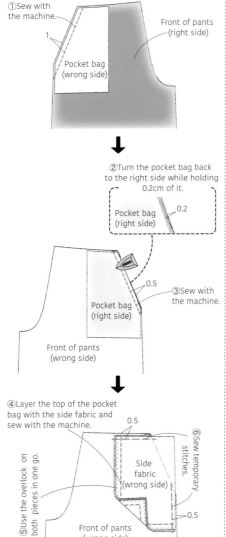

②Turn the pocket bag back
to the right side while holding
0.2cm of it.

Pocket bag
(right side)

0.2

0.5

③Sew with
the machine.

Pocket bag
(right side)

Front of pants
(wrong side)

④Layer the top of the pocket
bag with the side fabric and
sew with the machine.

0.5

⑤Use the overlock on
both pieces in one go.

Side
fabric
(wrong side)

⑥Sew temporary
stitches.

0.5

Front of pants
(wrong side)

※Create the other side in the same manner.

3. Sew the side line/inseam

Back of pants
(right side)

Pocket bag
(wrong side)

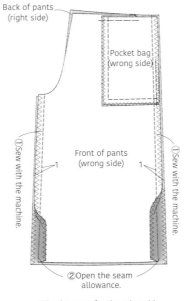

①Sew with the machine.

Front of pants
(wrong side)

1

1

①Sew with the machine.

②Open the seam
allowance.

※Do the same for the other side.

4. Sew the rise

①Turn one side over to the right side
and insert it into the other side.

Front of pants
(wrong side)

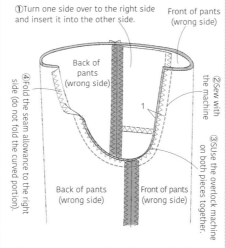

Back of
pants
(wrong side)

②Sew with
the machine

1

③Use the overlock machine
on both pieces together.

④Fold the seam allowance to the right
side (do not fold the curved portion).

Back of pants
(wrong side)

Front of pants
(wrong side)

5. Create a waist belt and attach it

①Fold and make a crease
as ironing in the finished
product

Waist belt
(right side)

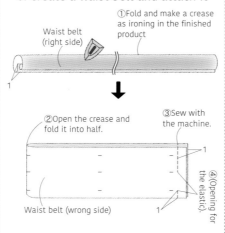

1

②Open the crease and
fold it into half.

③Sew with
the machine.

④Opening for
the elastic.

1

Waist belt (wrong side)

1

6. [Waist belt attachment]

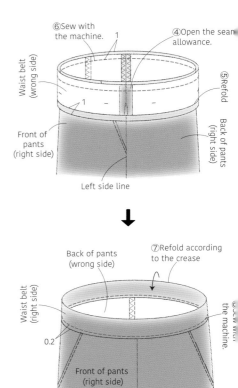

⑥Sew with
the machine.

1

④Open the seam
allowance.

Waist belt
(wrong side)

⑤Refold

Front of
pants
(right side)

Back of
pants
(right side)

Left side line

Back of pants
(wrong side)

⑦Refold according
to the crease

Waist belt
(right side)

0.2

Front of pants
(right side)

6. Finishing

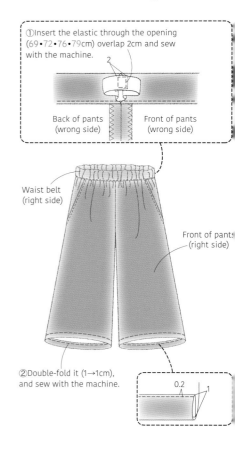

①Insert the elastic through the opening
(69・72・76・79cm) overlap 2cm and sew
with the machine.

2

Back of pants
(wrong side)

Front of pants
(wrong side)

Waist belt
(right side)

Front of pants
(right side)

②Double-fold it (1→1cm),
and sew with the machine.

0.2

1

P.47 No.29 Salopette

Materials

	S	M	L	LL
Outer fabric 146cm wide (Corduroy)	1.7m	1.8m	2m	2m
Other fabric 50cm wide (Sheeting)	35cm			
Adhesive tape (flat) 1cm wide	2.1m			
Adhesive tape (half-bias) 1cm wide	1.7m			
Double-folded bias tape 1.2cm wide	3.3m			

Sizing

	S	M	L	LL
Bust	90cm	94cm	98cm	103cm
Hip	113cm	119cm	125cm	130cm
Total length	123.5cm	127cm	130cm	133cm

Full-scale pattern	Side D

About the pattern

※Use the pattern for the body from No.24 and No.25, and the pants from No.27 and No.27.

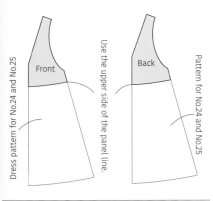

Construction Order

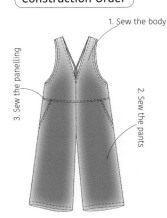

1. Sew the body
2. Sew the pants
3. Sew the panelling

How to cut the fabric

※If not specified (figure stated inside the ●), a 1cm seam allowance should be added.

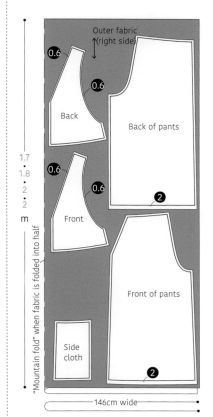

Outer fabric (right side)

Back

Back of pants

Front

Front of pants

Side cloth

"Mountain fold" when fabric is folded into half

1.7 · 1.8 · 2 · 2 m

146cm wide

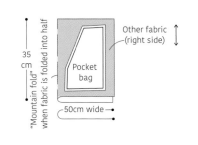

Other fabric (right side)

Pocket bag

35 cm

"Mountain fold" when fabric is folded into half

50cm wide

1. Sew the body

①Refer to page 82 and 83, steps 1 to 4 to sew the body.

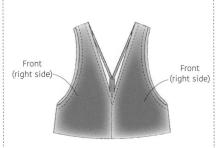

Front (right side)

Front (right side)

2. Sew the pants

①Refer to page 84, steps 1 to 4

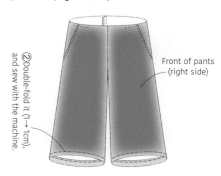

②Double-fold it (1 → 1cm), and sew with the machine.

Front of pants (right side)

3. Sew the paneling line

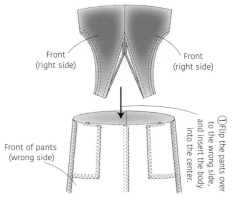

Front (right side)

Front (right side)

Front of pants (wrong side)

①Flip the pants over to the wrong side, and insert the body into the center.

③Use the overlock machine on both pieces at the same time.

Back (wrong side)

②Align with the panel line and sew with the machine.

1

Align the front and back centerline and the side line

Front of pants (wrong side)

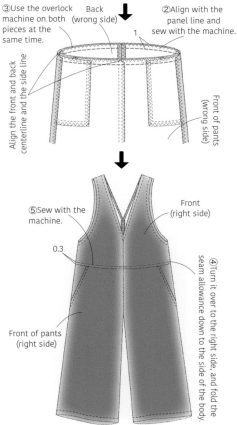

⑤Sew with the machine.

0.3

Front (right side)

Front of pants (right side)

④Turn it over to the right side, and fold the seam allowance down to the side of the body.

P.46 No.28 Tucked Pants

Materials

	S	M	L	LL
Outer fabric 144cm wide (T/R Raised Fabric)	2m	2m	2m	2.1m
Interfacing 50cm wide	10cm			
Rubber tape 3cm wide	50cm			

Sizing

	S	M	L	LL
Waist	70cm	74cm	78cm	82cm
Hip	116cm	122cm	130cm	136cm
Total length	88cm	90cm	95cm	94cm

Full-scale pattern Side B

How to cut the fabric

※If not specified (figure stated inside the ●), a 1cm seam allowance should be added.

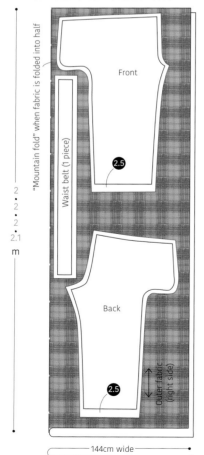

"Mountain fold" when fabric is folded into half

Front

Waist belt (1 piece)

2.5

2
·
2
·
2
·
2
·
2.1
m

Back

2.5

Outer fabric (right side)

← 144cm wide →

Construction Order

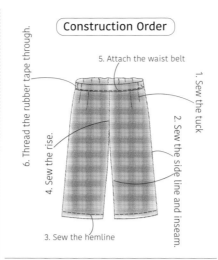

5. Attach the waist belt

6. Thread the rubber tape through.

4. Sew the rise.

1. Sew the tuck

2. Sew the side line and inseam.

3. Sew the hemline

---

1. Sew the tuck

①Fold the tucks and sew temporary stitches with the sewing machine

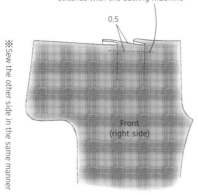

0.5

Front (right side)

※Sew the other side in the same manner

---

2. Sew the side line and the inseam

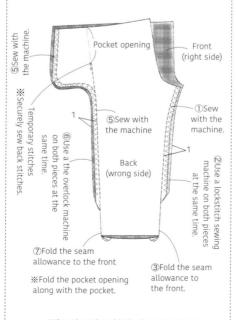

⑤Sew with the machine.

Pocket opening

Front (right side)

①Sew with the machine.

※Securely sew back stitches.

Temporary stitches

⑤Sew with the machine

⑥Use a the overlock machine on both pieces at the same time.

1

Back (wrong side)

②Use a lockstitch sewing machine on both pieces at the same time.

1

⑦Fold the seam allowance to the front

※Fold the pocket opening along with the pocket.

③Fold the seam allowance to the front.

※Sew the other side in the same manner.

---

3. Sew the hemline

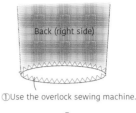

Back (right side)

①Use the overlock sewing machine.

↓

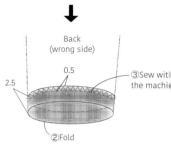

Back (wrong side)

0.5

2.5

③Sew with the machine

②Fold

※Sew the other side in the same manner

---

4. Sew the rise

①Turn it over to one side and insert it into the other.

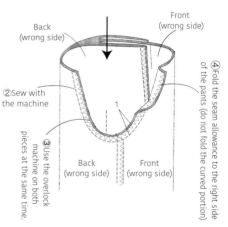

Back (wrong side)

Front (wrong side)

②Sew with the machine

④Fold the seam allowance to the right side of the pants (do not fold the curved portion)

③Use the overlock machine on both pieces at the same time.

1

Back (wrong side)

Front (wrong side)

---

5. Attach a waist belt

①On the front side, attach the interfacing up to where the elastic tape ends.

Waist belt (wrong side)

②Sew with a machine.

1

End of the elastic tape

③Press open the seam allowance.

↓

"Mountain fold" when fabric is folded into half

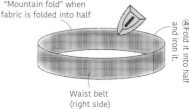

④Fold it into half and iron it.

Waist belt (right side)

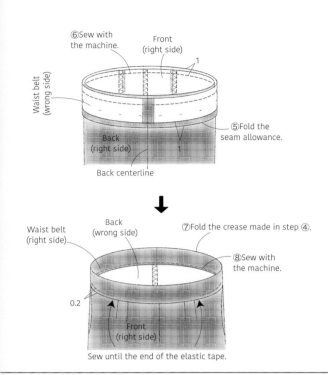

⑥Sew with the machine.

Front (right side)

1

Waist belt (wrong side)

Back (right side)

⑤Fold the seam allowance.

Back centerline

↓

Waist belt (right side)

Back (wrong side)

⑦Fold the crease made in step ④.

⑧Sew with the machine.

0.2

Front (right side)

Sew until the end of the elastic tape.

6. Thread the elastic tape through

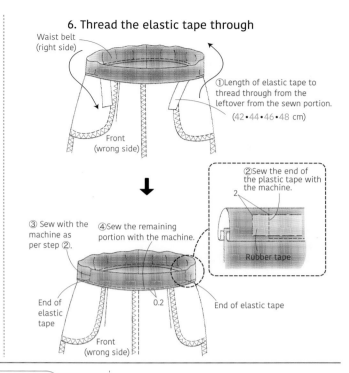

Waist belt (right side)

①Length of elastic tape to thread through from the leftover from the sewn portion.
(42・44・46・48 cm)

Front (wrong side)

↓

③ Sew with the machine as per step ②.

④Sew the remaining portion with the machine.

②Sew the end of the plastic tape with the machine.

2

Rubber tape

End of elastic tape

End of elastic tape

0.2

Front (wrong side)

No. 42   No. 43

P.57 No.42 Snood
P.57 No.43 Snood

Materials

Outer fabric 110-150cm wide (Boa/Wool)	60cm

Sizing

Circumference	98cm	Length	27cm

Construction Order

2. Align with the back center point and sew.

1. Sew around

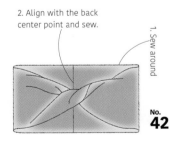

No. 42

No. 43

※Create No.43 in the same manner

How to cut the fabric

※There is no full-size pattern. Please cut directly to the dimensions listed.
※Cut every (seam allowance included).

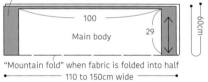

Outer fabric (right side)

100

Main body

29

60cm

"Mountain fold" when fabric is folded into half

110 to 150cm wide

1. Sew around

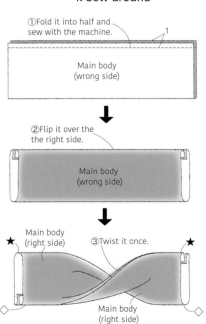

①Fold it into half and sew with the machine.

1

Main body (wrong side)

↓

②Flip it over the the right side.

Main body (wrong side)

↓

★ Main body (right side)   ③Twist it once.   ★

◇   Main body (right side)   ◇

---

2. Align with the back center point and sew

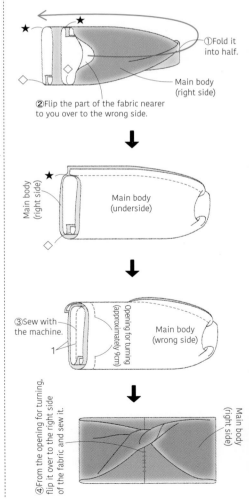

★   ★

①Fold it into half.

Main body (right side)

②Flip the part of the fabric nearer to you over to the wrong side.

↓

★

Main body (right side)

Main body (underside)

◇

↓

③Sew with the machine.

1

Main body (right side)

Opening for turning (approximately 9cm)

Main body (wrong side)

↓

④From the opening for turning, flip it over to the right side of the fabric and sew it.

Main body (right side)

85

No. 30 No. 31

P.48, 49 No.30, No.31 Tucked Skirt

Materials

	M	LL
Outer fabric 135/110cm wide (Corduroy Shirting/ Compressed Wool)	1.6m	1.7m
Rubber tape 1.5cm wide	70cm	

Sizing

	M	LL
Waist	60cm	66cm
Total length	69cm	72.5cm

About the pattern

※There is no full-scale pattern. Please use the following image.
※Dimensions for ■...M ■...LL
(■ is uniform across all sizes).

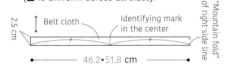

Belt cloth   Identifying mark in the center

2.5 cm

"Mountain fold" of right side line

46.2・51.8 cm

★···3.4・3.7 cm ☆···6.6・7.4 cm   3.3・3.7 cm

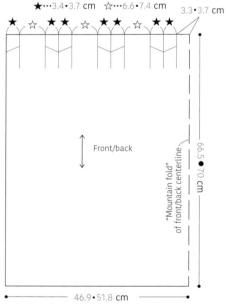

Front/back

"Mountain fold" of front/back centerline

66.5・70 cm

46.9・51.8 cm

How to pleat the tuck

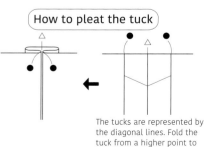

The tucks are represented by the diagonal lines. Fold the tuck from a higher point to a lower point.

How to cut fabric

※If not specified (figure stated inside the ●), a 1cm seam allowance should be added.

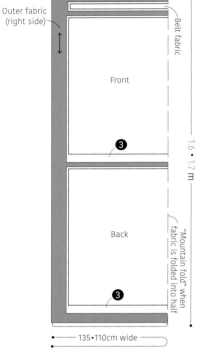

Outer fabric (right side)

Belt fabric

Front

❸

Back

❸

1.6・1.7 m

"Mountain fold" when fabric is folded into half

135・110cm wide

Construction Order   No. 30

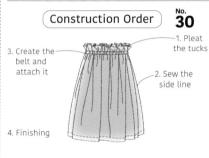

3. Create the belt and attach it

1. Pleat the tucks

2. Sew the side line

4. Finishing

※Create No.31 in the same manner.

1. Pleat the tucks

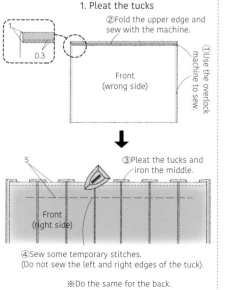

②Fold the upper edge and sew with the machine.

0.3

1

①Use the overlock machine to sew.

Front (wrong side)

5

③Pleat the tucks and iron the middle.

Front (right side)

④Sew some temporary stitches.
(Do not sew the left and right edges of the tuck).

※Do the same for the back.

---

2. Sew the side lines

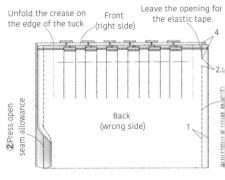

Unfold the crease on the edge of the tuck

Front (right side)

Leave the opening for the elastic tape.

4

②Press open seam allowance

Back (wrong side)

1

3. Create a waist belt and attach it

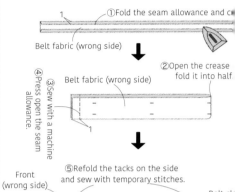

①Fold the seam allowance and c(...)

Belt fabric (wrong side)

②Open the crease fold it into half

④Press open the seam allowance.

③Sew with a machine

Belt fabric (wrong side)

1

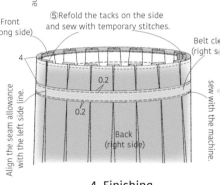

Front (wrong side)

⑤Refold the tacks on the side and sew with temporary stitches.

Belt cl(...) (right s(...)

4

0.2

0.2

Back (right side)

sew with the machine.

Align the seam allowance with the left side line.

4. Finishing

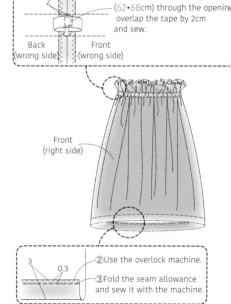

2

①Thread the elastic tape (62・68cm) through the openin(...) overlap the tape by 2cm and sew.

Back (wrong side) Front (wrong side)

Front (right side)

3   0.2

②Use the overlock machine.

③Fold the seam allowance and sew it with the machine.

P.50, 51 No.32, No.33
Gathered Button Front Skirt

Materials

	S	M	L	LL
Outer fabric 134/110cm wide	1.8m	1.8m	1.8m	1.9m
Interfacing 90cm wide	1m			
Button 1.8cm wide	6 pieces			

Sizing

	S	M	L	LL
Waist	70cm	74cm	77.5cm	81.5cm
Total length	75cm	77cm	79cm	82cm

About the pattern

※There is no full-scale dress. Please use the image below.
※Dimensions for ■…S ■…M ■…L ■…LL (■ is uniform across all sizes).

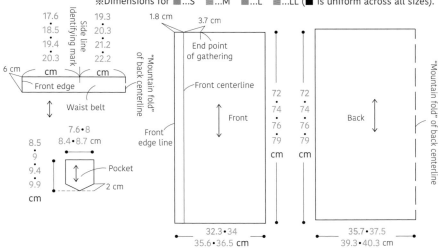

How to cut the fabric

※If not specified (figure stated inside the ●), a 1cm seam allowance should be added.
※▦ denotes the part for attaching the interfacing (please refer to page 60).

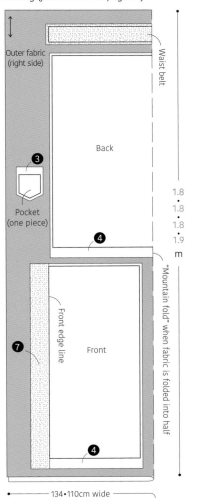

Construction Order

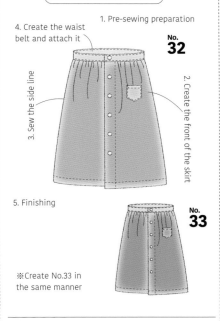

1. Pre-sewing preparation
2. Create the front of the skirt
3. Sew the side line
4. Create the waist belt and attach it
5. Finishing

No. 32

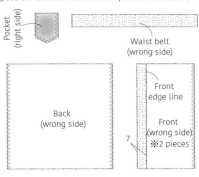

No. 33

※Create No.33 in the same manner

1. Pre-sewing preparation

① ▦ denotes the part for attaching the interfacing (please refer to .page 60).
②Use the overlock machine the portion marked 〜〜

Pocket (right side)
Waist belt (wrong side)
Back (wrong side)
Front edge line
Front (wrong side) ※2 pieces

2. Create the front of the skirt

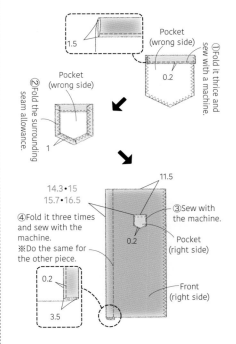

①Fold it thrice and sew with a machine.
②Fold the surrounding seam allowance.
③Sew with the machine.
④Fold it three times and sew with the machine.
※Do the same for the other piece.

Pocket (wrong side)
Pocket (right side)
Front (right side)

3. Sew the side lines

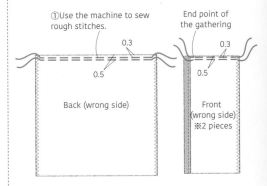

①Use the machine to sew rough stitches.

End point of the gathering

Back (wrong side)
Front (wrong side) ※2 pieces

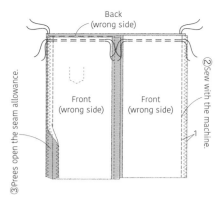

③Press open the seam allowance.

Back (wrong side)

Front (wrong side)

Front (wrong side)

②Sew with the machine.

1

1

4. Create the waist belt and attach it

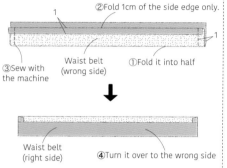

②Fold 1cm of the side edge only.

1

1

Waist belt (wrong side)

①Fold it into half

③Sew with the machine

Waist belt (right side)

④Turn it over to the wrong side

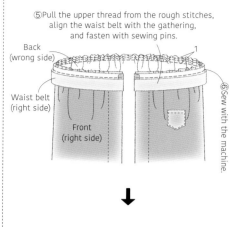

⑤Pull the upper thread from the rough stitches, align the waist belt with the gathering, and fasten with sewing pins.

Back (wrong side)

1

Waist belt (right side)

Front (right side)

⑥Sew with the machine.

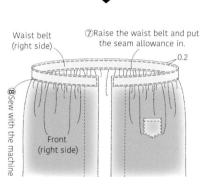

Waist belt (right side)

⑦Raise the waist belt and put the seam allowance in.

0.2

⑧Sew with the machine

Front (right side)

5. Finishing

①Open the buttonhole

1.5

0.3

Length of buttonhole = width of buttonhole + thickness of buttonhole

Position of button

Front centerline

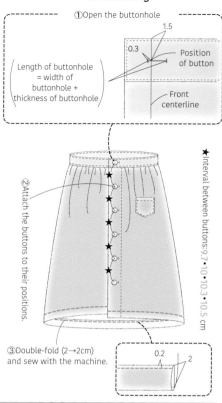

②Attach the buttons to their positions.

★Interval between buttons: 9.7•10•10.3•10.5 cm

③Double-fold (2→2cm) and sew with the machine.

0.2   2

No. 34

P.52 No.34 Elbow-Length Pullover

Materials

Outer fabric 140cm wide (Wool Knit)	1.2m
Interfacing 90cm wide	15cm

Sizing(Free-Size)

Bust	158cm
Total length	54.5cm

※There is no full-scale pattern.
Please use the image on page 91 to create it.

Construction Order

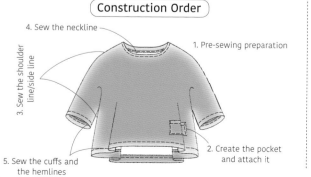

4. Sew the neckline

1. Pre-sewing preparation

3. Sew the shoulder line/side line

5. Sew the cuffs and the hemlines

2. Create the pocket and attach it

How to cut the fabric

※If not specified (figure stated inside the ●), a 1.5 cm seam allowance should be added.

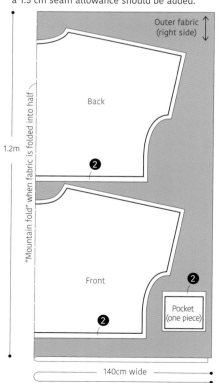

Outer fabric (right side)

"Mountain fold" when fabric is folded into half

1.2m

Back

❷

Front

❷

❷

Pocket (one piece)

❷

140cm wide

※There is no full-scale pattern. Please use this diagram.

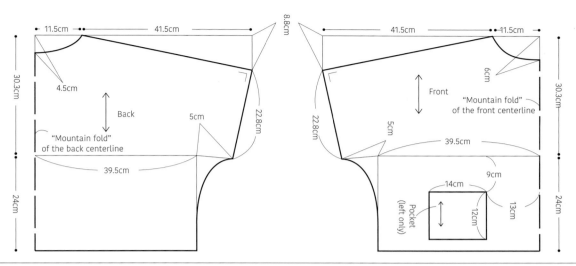

11.5cm — 41.5cm — 8.8cm — 41.5cm — 11.5cm

4.5cm — 6cm

30.3cm / 24cm (left side)

Back

"Mountain fold" of the back centerline

5cm — 22.8cm — 22.8cm — 5cm

39.5cm — 39.5cm

Front

"Mountain fold" of the front centerline

30.3cm / 24cm (right side)

9cm

14cm — 12cm — 13cm

Pocket (left only)

1. Pre-sewing preparation

①Stick horizontal interfacing on the armhole, neckline, hemline and opening of the pockets. Stick a vertical interfacing on the front of the shoulder line (please refer to page 60)

▨ Horizontal interfacing
▨ Vertical interfacing

Pocket (wrong side)

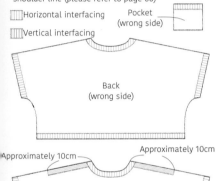

Back (wrong side)

Approximately 10cm — Approximately 10cm

Front (wrong side)

②Use the overlock machine on the shoulder line, and around the pocket.

Pocket (right side)

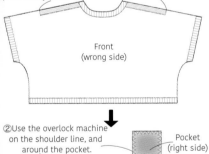

Back (right side)

Front (right side)

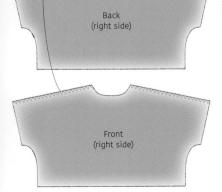

2. Create the pocket and attach it

②Fold the seam allowance.

①Fold and sew with the machine.

2

Pocket (wrong side)

0.3

Pocket (wrong side)

1.5

Pocket (wrong side)

1.5

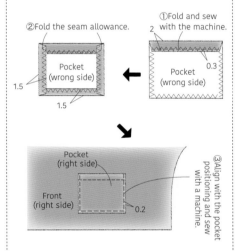

Pocket (right side)

Front (right side)

0.2

③Align with the pocket positioning and sew with a machine.

3. Sew the shoulder line and side line

②Press open the seam allowance.

Back (right side)

①Sew with the machine.

1.5

③Sew with the machine

Front (wrong side)

1.5

⑤Fold the seam allowance to the back.

④Use the overlock machine on both pieces together.

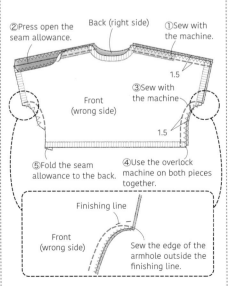

Finishing line

Front (wrong side)

Sew the edge of the armhole outside the finishing line.

4. Sew the neckline

Back (wrong side)

①Use the overlock machine

Front (right side)

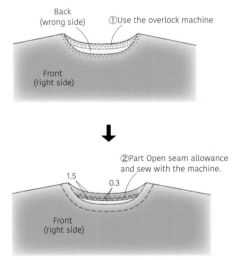

②Part Open seam allowance and sew with the machine.

1.5 — 0.3

Front (right side)

5. Sew the armhole and the hemline

Back (wrong side)

Front (right side)

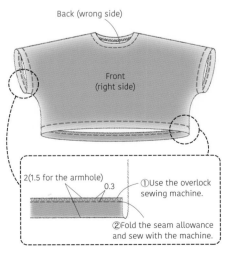

2(1.5 for the armhole)

0.3

①Use the overlock sewing machine.

②Fold the seam allowance and sew with the machine.

P.53 No.35
Rolled-Collar Knit Dress
Materials

	S	M	L
Outer fabric 135cm wide (Wool Nylon Knit)	1.7m	1.7m	1.7m
Interfacing 90cm wide		20cm	

Sizing

	S	M	L
Bust	102cm	108cm	114cm
Total length	52cm	53cm	54cm

P.53 No.36
Rolled-Collar Knit Pullover
Materials

	S	M	L
Outer Fabric 140cm wide (Wool Nylon Knit)	2.3m	2.3m	2.3m
Interfacing 90cm wide		20cm	

Sizing

	S	M	L
Bust	102cm	108cm	114cm
Total length	81cm	82cm	83cm

Construction Order

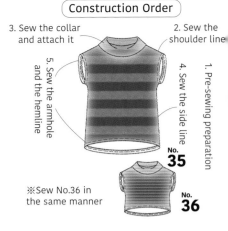

3. Sew the collar and attach it
2. Sew the shoulder line
5. Sew the armhole and the hemline
4. Sew the side line
1. Pre-sewing preparation

No.
35

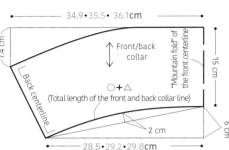

※Sew No.36 in the same manner

No.
36

34.9・35.5・36.1cm

7.4 cm

15 cm

6 cm

"Mountain fold" of the front centerline

Front/back collar

Back centerline

○+△
(Total length of the front and back collar line)

2 cm

28.5・29.2・29.8cm

※There is no full-scale pattern. Please use this image.
※Dimensions for ■...S ■...M ■...L (■ is uniform across all sizes)

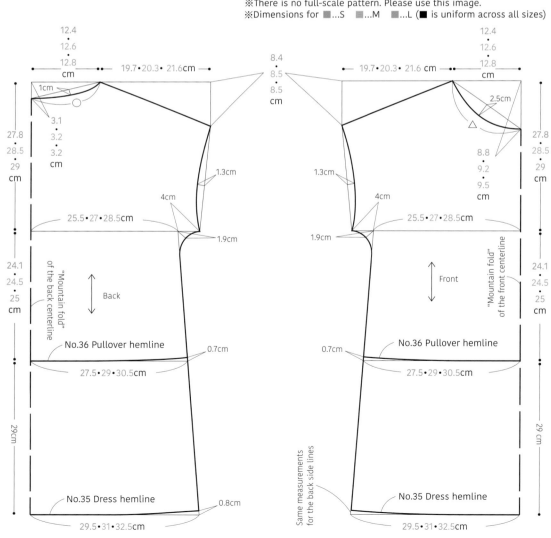

12.4・12.6・12.8 cm

19.7・20.3・21.6cm

1cm

27.8・28.5・29 cm

3.1・3.2・3.2 cm

1.3cm

25.5・27・28.5cm

4cm

1.9cm

24.1・24.5・25 cm

"Mountain fold" of the back centerline

Back

No.36 Pullover hemline

0.7cm

27.5・29・30.5cm

29cm

No.35 Dress hemline

0.8cm

29.5・31・32.5cm

8.4・8.5・8.5 cm

19.7・20.3・21.6 cm

12.4・12.6・12.8 cm

2.5cm

27.8・28.5・29 cm

8.8・9.2・9.5 cm

1.3cm

1.9cm

4cm

25.5・27・28.5cm

24.1・24.5・25 cm

"Mountain fold" of the front centerline

Front

No.36 Pullover hemline

0.7cm

27.5・29・30.5cm

29 cm

Same measurements for the back side lines

No.35 Dress hemline

29.5・31・32.5cm

90

How to cut the fabric

If not specified (figure stated inside the ●),
1cm seam allowance should be added.

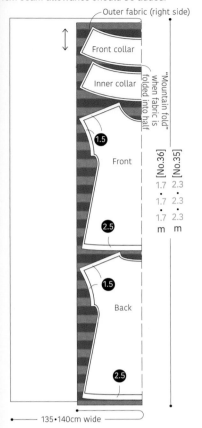

Outer fabric (right side)

Front collar

Inner collar

"Mountain fold"
when fabric is
folded into half

Front

●1.5

●2.5

Back

●1.5

●2.5

[No.36]	[No.35]
1.7	2.3
1.7	2.3
1.7	2.3
m	m

135·140cm wide

1. Pre-sewing preparation

tick horizontal interfacings on the armhole and hemline.
ck vertical interfacings on the front shoulder line
ase refer to age 60)

Approximately
10cm

Approximately
10cm

Horizontal interfacing
Vertical interfacing

Front
(wrong side)

Back
(wrong side)

---

②Use the overlock machine on the ～～ portion marked

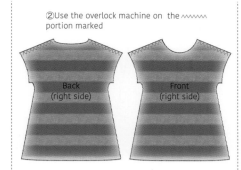

Back
(right side)

Front
(right side)

2. Sew the shoulder line

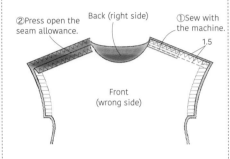

②Press open the
seam allowance.

Back (right side)

①Sew with
the machine.

1.5

Front
(wrong side)

3. Create the collar and attach it

※Sew the under collar in the same manner.

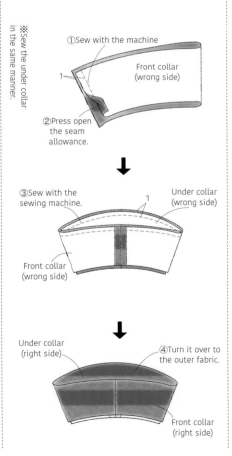

①Sew with the machine

Front collar
(wrong side)

1

②Press open
the seam
allowance.

③Sew with the
sewing machine.

Under collar
(wrong side)

1

Front collar
(wrong side)

Under collar
(right side)

④Turn it over to
the outer fabric.

Front collar
(right side)

---

⑥Use the overlock
machine on 3
pieces together.

1

⑤Sew with the machine

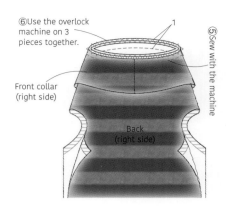

Front collar
(right side)

Back
(right side)

4.Sew the side line

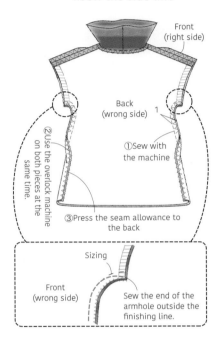

Front
(right side)

②Use the overlock machine
on both pieces at the
same time.

Back
(wrong side)

1

①Sew with
the machine

③Press the seam allowance to
the back

Sizing

Front
(wrong side)

Sew the end of the
armhole outside the
finishing line.

5. Sew the armhole and the hemline

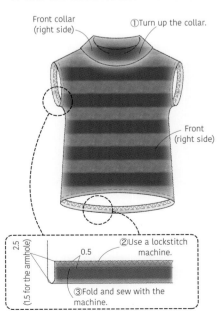

Front collar
(right side)

①Turn up the collar.

Front
(right side)

2.5
(1.5 for the armhole)

0.5

②Use a lockstitch
machine.

③Fold and sew with the
machine.

No. 37

P.54 No.37 Marguerite

Materials

Outer fabric 140cm wide (Wool Polyester Knit)	1m
Interfacing 90cm wide	10cm

Sizing(Free Size)

Total length	Approximately 90cm

How to cut the fabric

※Use the figures stated inside the
● for the seam allowance.

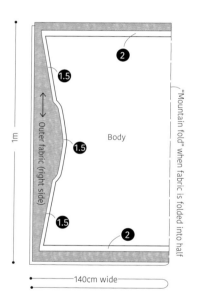

Construction Order

1. Pre-sewing preparation

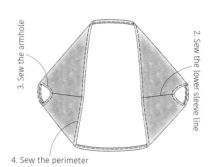

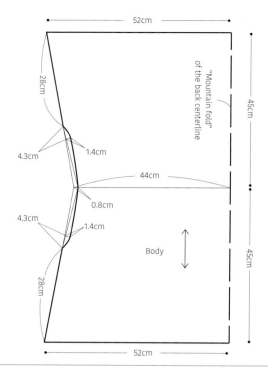

※There is no full-scale pattern. Please use the image.

---

1. Pre-sewing preparation

①Stick the horizontal interfacing on the armhole and hemlines (please refer to page 60).
②Use the overlock the portion marked ∧∧∧∧

▦ Horizontal interfacing

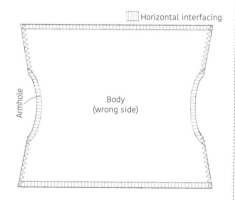

2. Sew the lower sleeve line

①Fold it into half.

③Press open the seam allowance. ②Sew with the machine.

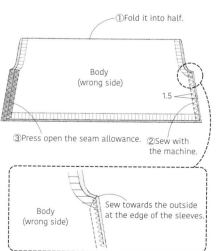

Sew towards the outside at the edge of the sleeves.

3. Sew the armhole

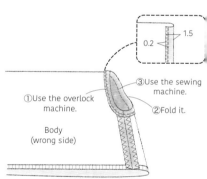

①Use the overlock machine.
②Fold it.
③Use the sewing machine.

4. Sew the perimeter

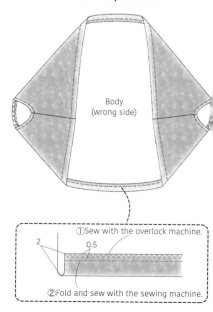

①Sew with the overlock machine.
②Fold and sew with the sewing machine.

No.
35

P.54 No.38 Short Cardigan

Materials

Outer fabric 200cm wide (Wool Knit)	70cm

Sizing (Free Size)

Total length	60cm	Bust	120cm

※There is no full-scale pattern.
Please use the following image.

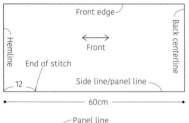

Front edge
Hemline
Front
Back centerline
End of stitch
Side line/panel line
12
60cm

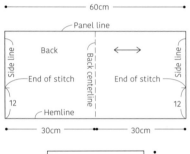

Panel line
Side line
Back
Back centerline
Side line
End of stitch
End of stitch
12
Hemline
12
30cm
30cm

Cuff
8cm
36cm

1. Pre-sewing preparation

Paste the horizontal facing on the back centerline on the front (please refer to page 60).

║║ Vertical interfacing

Front
(wrong side)
※2 pieces
Back centerline

②Use the ovelock machine around the fabric pieces.

Front
(right side)
※2 pieces
Selvedge

Back
(right side)

Construction Order

1. Pre-sewing preparation

2. Sew the back centerline

3. Sew the panel line and the side line

5. Sew the neckline to the hemline

4. Create the cuffs and attach it

How to cut the fabric

※If not specified (figure stated inside the ●), a 1cm seam allowance should be added.

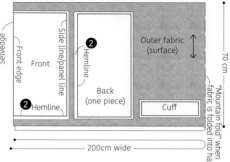

Selvedge
Front edge
Side line/panel line
Front
❷
Hemline
Outer fabric (surface)
❷ Hemline
Back (one piece)
Cuff
70 cm
"Mountain fold" when fabric is folded into half
200cm wide

---

2. Sew the back centerline

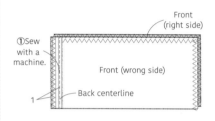

Front (right side)
①Sew with a machine.
Front (wrong side)
1
Back centerline

3. Sew the panel line and side line

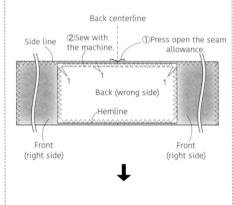

Back centerline
Side line
②Sew with the machine.
①Press open the seam allowance.
1
1
Back (wrong side)
Hemline
Front (right side)
Front (right side)

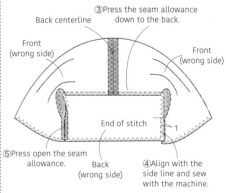

③Press the seam allowance down to the back.
Back centerline
Front (wrong side)
Front (wrong side)
End of stitch
1
⑤Press open the seam allowance.
Back (wrong side)
④Align with the side line and sew with the machine.

---

4. Create the cuff and attach it

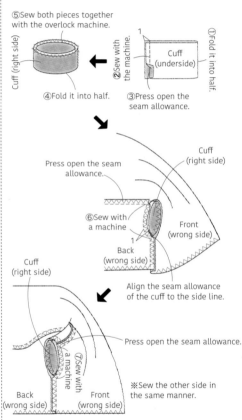

⑤Sew both pieces together with the overlock machine.
Cuff (right side)
②Sew with the machine.
1
Cuff (underside)
①Fold it into half.
④Fold it into half.
③Press open the seam allowance.
Press open the seam allowance.
Cuff (right side)
⑥Sew with a machine.
1
Front (wrong side)
Back (wrong side)
Cuff (right side)
Align the seam allowance of the cuff to the side line.
Press open the seam allowance.
Back (wrong side)
⑦Sew with a machine
Front (wrong side)
※Sew the other side in the same manner.

5. Sew the neckline to the hemline

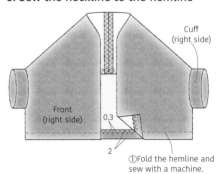

Cuff (right side)
Front (right side)
0.3
2
①Fold the hemline and sew with a machine.

93

Construction Order

3. Sew the back centerline of the collar

1. Pre-sewing preparation

4. Sew the panel line and side line

2. Create the pocket and attach it (only No.40)

No. 40

6. Finishing

No. 41

※Sew No.41 in the same manner

P.56 No.41 Robe Jacket

Materials

	S	M	L
Outer fabric 130cm wide (Cotton Wool)	2m	2m	2.1m
Interfacing 20cm wide	10cm		

Sizing

	S	M	L
Bust	102cm	108cm	114cm
Total length	about 59cm	about 60cm	about 61cm

P.56 No.40 Robe Coat

Materials

	S	M	L
Outer fabric 145cm wide (Jazz Nep Wool)	2.5m	2.5m	2.6m
Interfacing 20cm wide	10cm		

Sizing

	S	M	L
Bust	102cm	108cm	114cm
Total length	about 111cm	about 113cm	about 115cm

※There is no full-scale pattern. Please use the following image.

※Dimensions for ■...S ■...M ■...L (■ is uniform across all sizes).

※After drawing, please ensure that the measurements for each adjoining part (shoulder line, side line, armhole) are the same.

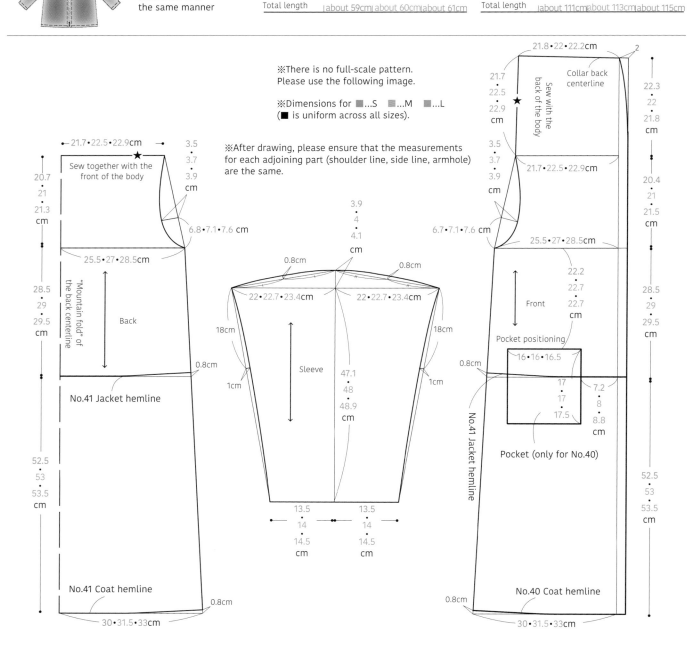

Back piece (left): 21.7·22.5·22.9cm; Sew together with the front of the body ★; 20.7·21·21.3cm; 3.5·3.7·3.9cm; 6.8·7.1·7.6cm; 25.5·27·28.5cm; 28.5·29·29.5cm; "Mountain fold" of the back centerline; Back; No.41 Jacket hemline; 0.8cm; 52.5·53·53.5cm; No.41 Coat hemline; 0.8cm; 30·31.5·33cm

Sleeve (center): 3.9·4·4.1cm; 0.8cm; 0.8cm; 22·22.7·23.4cm; 22·22.7·23.4cm; 18cm; 18cm; Sleeve; 47.1·48·48.9cm; 1cm; 1cm; 13.5·14·14.5cm; 13.5·14·14.5cm

Front piece (right): 21.8·22·22.2cm; 2; Collar back centerline; Sew with the back of the body; 21.7·22.5·22.9cm; 22.3·22·21.8cm; 3.5·3.7·3.9cm; 6.7·7.1·7.6cm; 21.7·22.5·22.9cm; 20.4·21·21.5cm; 25.5·27·28.5cm; 22.2·22.7·22.7cm; Front; 28.5·29·29.5cm; Pocket positioning; 16·16·16.5cm; 17·17·17.5cm; 7.2·8·8.8cm; 0.8cm; No.41 Jacket hemline; Pocket (only for No.40); 52.5·53·53.5cm; No.40 Coat hemline; 0.8cm; 30·31.5·33cm

[How to cut the fabric]

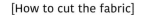

※If not specified (figure stated inside the ●), a 1cm seam allowance should be added.

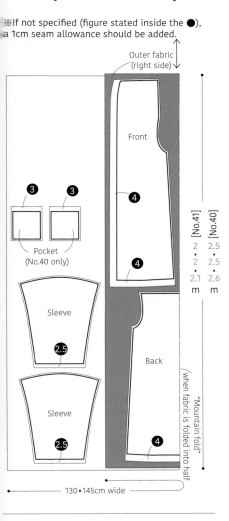

Outer fabric (right side)

Front

❸ ❸
Pocket (No.40 only)

❹

❹

Sleeve
②.⑤

Sleeve
②.⑤

❹

Back

"Mountain fold" (when fabric is folded into half)

	[No.41]	[No.40]
	2	2.5
	2	2.5
	2.1	2.6
	m	m

130・145cm wide

1. Pre-sewing preparation

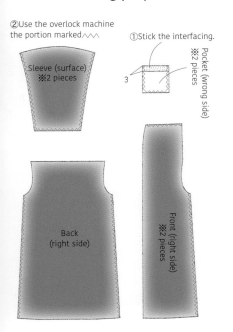

②Use the overlock machine the portion marked ∧∧∧

①Stick the interfacing.
※2 pieces

Sleeve (surface) ※2 pieces

3

Pocket (wrong side) ※2 pieces

Back (right side)

Front (right side) ※2 pieces

2. Create the pocket and attach it (No.40 only)

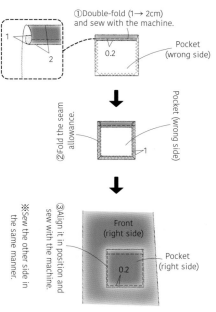

①Double-fold (1→2cm) and sew with the machine.

1
2
0.2
Pocket (wrong side)

②Fold the seam allowance.

Pocket (wrong side)
1

③Align it in position and sew with the machine.
※Sew the other side in the same manner.

Front (right side)

0.2

Pocket (right side)

3. Sew the back centerline of the collar

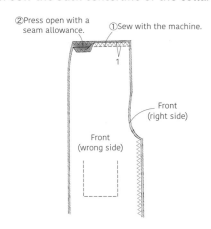

②Press open with a seam allowance.
①Sew with the machine.
1

Front (right side)

Front (wrong side)

4. Sew the panel line and side line

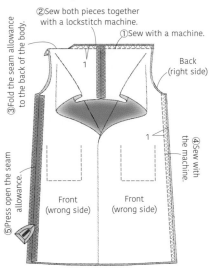

②Sew both pieces together with a lockstitch machine.
①Sew with a machine.
1

Back (right side)

③Fold the seam allowance to the back of the body.

1

④Sew with the machine.

⑤Press open the seam allowance.

Front (wrong side)
Front (wrong side)

5. Create the sleeve and attach it

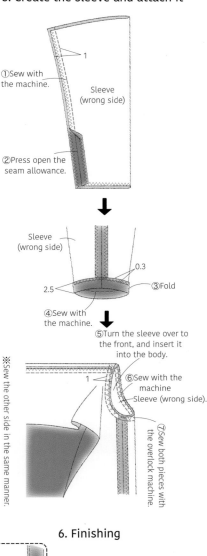

1
①Sew with the machine.

Sleeve (wrong side)

②Press open the seam allowance.

Sleeve (wrong side)

0.3
2.5
③Fold

④Sew with the machine.

⑤Turn the sleeve over to the front, and insert it into the body.

※Sew the other side in the same manner.

1
⑥Sew with the machine
Sleeve (wrong side).

⑦Sew both pieces with the overlock machine.

6. Finishing

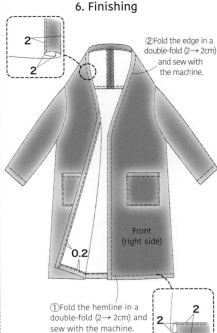

2
2

②Fold the edge in a double-fold (2→2cm) and sew with the machine.

Front (right side)

0.2

①Fold the hemline in a double-fold (2→2cm) and sew with the machine.

2
2

P.55 No.39 Ribbed Bolero

Materials

	S	M	L
Outer fabric 100cm wide (Wool Knit)	1.2m	1.2m	1.2m
Interfacing 90cm wide		10cm	

Sizing

	S	M	L
Width from the center of the neck to the end of the sleeve at the wrist	63cm	64cm	65cm
Total length	64cm	66cm	68cm

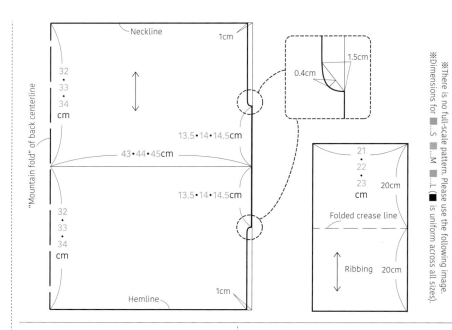

※There is no full-scale pattern. Please use the following image.
※Dimensions for ....S
....M
....L (■ is uniform across all sizes).

Neckline
1cm
1.5cm
0.4cm
32・33・34 cm
13.5・14・14.5cm
43・44・45cm
13.5・14・14.5cm
32・33・34 cm
1cm
Hemline
"Mountain fold" of back centerline
21・22・23 cm
20cm
Folded crease line
Ribbing 20cm

How to cut the fabric

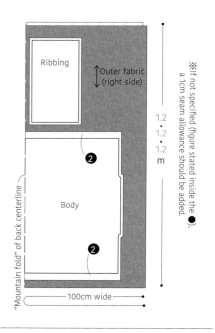

Ribbing

Outer fabric (right side)

Body

❷

❷

"Mountain fold" of back centerline

100cm wide

1.2・1.2・1.2 m

※If not specified (figure stated inside the ●), a 1cm seam allowance should be added.

Construction Order

1. Pre-sewing preparation

4. Sew from the neckline to the hemline

2. Sew the side line

3. Create the rib and attach it

1. Pre-sewing preparation

①Stick a horizontal interfacing on the neckline and the hemline (please refer to Page 60).

▨ Horizontal interfacing

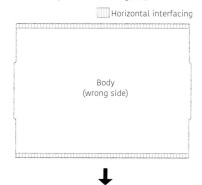

Body (wrong side)

②Use the overlock machine on the portion marked 〰

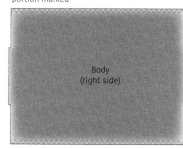

Body (right side)

2. Sew the side line

①Fold it into half.

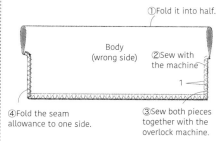

Body (wrong side)

②Sew with the machine

1

④Fold the seam allowance to one side.

③Sew both pieces together with the overlock machine.

3. Create the ribbing and attach it

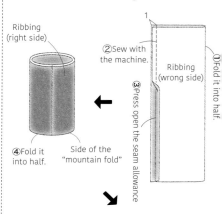

1

Ribbing (right side)

②Sew with the machine.

③Press open the seam allowance

①Fold it into half.

Ribbing (wrong side)

④Fold it into half.

Side of the "mountain fold"

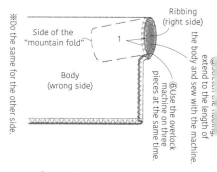

※Do the same for the other side.

Side of the "mountain fold"

1

Ribbing (right side)

Body (wrong side)

⑤Overlock the ribbing, extend to the length of the body and sew with the machine.

⑥Use the overlock machine on three pieces at the same time.

4. Sew from the neckline to the hemline

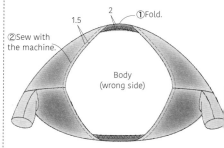

①Fold.

2

1.5

②Sew with the machine.

Body (wrong side)